JOURNEY TO JUSTICE

JOURNEY TO JUSTICE

R. GRACIE TRAVIS-MURPHREE

EQUIP PRESS

Colorado Springs

JOURNEY TO JUSTICE

First Edition: Year 2018
Journey to Justice /R. Gracie Travis-Murphree
Paperback ISBN: 978-1-946453-55-6
eBook ISBN: 978-1-946453-56-3

EQUIP PRESS

Colorado Springs

PRAISE FOR JOURNEY TO JUSTICE

"This book will rock your world and stir your soul. In Journey to Justice, Gracie Travis-Murphree pulls no punches as she details the trauma, violence, murder, corruption, and other third-world realities of Honduras. But the book is a journey to God's heart and his miraculous work through one inadequate servant. A challenging book that nurtures hope and invites the reader to go deeper in their justice journey."

—*Bruce D. Strom, CEO Gospel Justice Initiative &*
Administer Justice, Author Gospel Justice

"A warrior for justice armed with faith and determination, Gracie Murphree's account of her human rights work in Honduras must be read. It opened my mind and heart to the depth of the entrenched corruption in a society that fails to protect children and other populations. She is a force for women and girls in a society that has the highest femicide rate in the world. She brings alive the pain and sorrow of the struggling nation and yet, despite the violence and systemic corruption, her words are filled with faith in love and the power of the people to work together to live in peace. Her book inspires me to renew my commitment to aiding Hondurans who flee systemic violence and seek refuge status, but more, her book should call all of us to act. With collective action we can bring change."

—*Lenni B. Benson, Professor of Law, Director Safe Passage Project*
Clinic, New York Law School

"Journey to Justice: Finding God and Destiny in Darkness is exactly what Gracie shows us in this fiercely empowering testimony of her journey to salvation and her experiences on the mission field. It is a riveting read, some of it in anguish at dark, sin nature of the offenders, some at God's unfailing grace and mercy despite the darkness. The book is an emotional storm, much like her journey."

—*John Hall,* Executive Director Ezra821.org

"Captivating. Heart breaking. Inspiring. Gracie's story is a testimony of obedience, and evidence of just how much God can do with a life that says 'Yes' and is surrendered to Him. Journey to Justice and the mission of Heart of Christ have the fingerprints of Jesus all over them."

—*Diana Chaloux-LaCerte,* Author, Entrepreneur, Co-Owner Hitch Fit

"Gracie's story is a portrait of true faith, one that follows her and her husband Lee as they make a life-changing move to start a mission in the mountains of Honduras, one of the world's most dangerous countries. As you read about their determined efforts, you will be moved, astonished, and humbled. They don't preach empty words, but are living examples of the power of love, as taught at the very beginnings of Christianity. In the face of apathy, in the face of opposition, and in the face of grave danger, they have created a safe haven for women and children at risk and have begun to change Honduras into a less-dangerous country."

—*Jennifer Greenhill-Taylor,* Writer and Editor

"Often I cry out Habbakuk that the 'law has become paralyzed, and there is no justice in the courts' here in Honduras. But God has sent Gracie and Lee with love and determination to extend their hands to those least able to defend themselves. The story of their journey is truly a light of hope."

—**Kathy Brown,** *Cofounder Cultivate Honduras*

"Reading about Journey to Justice may make you wonder if you've gotten ahold of a movie script, but there's nothing fictional about Gracie Murphree's experience as a missionary in Honduras, murder capital of the world. Her account of the ministry she and her husband, Lee, started is as incredible as it is inspirational. These are true stories she tells about striving for justice in a place where it's not very common, where people suffer unimaginable violence every day. But she and Lee are determined to seek justice for those who cannot seek it for themselves, and to help keep them safe in the process. The book answers the question about whether just one person can make a difference. That answer is an unqualified 'yes.'"

—**Amy Pollick,** *Staff Writer DealNews.com*

DEDICATION

For my Savior, for if it were not for his grace in me, none of this would have happened.

To all the courageous men and women who fight for peace and justice in Honduras and around the world.

CONTENTS

WOULD IT MAKE A DIFFERENCE?

Music and writing have always been my means of coping and of celebrating. Living in darkness among violence, rape, and murder isn't easy. By choosing to leave everything behind to live and work for justice in Honduras, I have had to desperately cling to my faith and prayer, submerge myself in worship music, and pour out my emotions on the page to survive and continue this challenging journey.

There have been many times since 2005, when we began this work rescuing women and children from violence, that my husband, Lee, and I have experienced such anguish and torment and come to the end of our endurance, we considered walking away from it all. It was too hard, too ugly, too overwhelming. It was in those moments when we turned to prayer and discovered, during our moments of weakness, that God was able to step into this darkness and make a way, to give us strength to take the next step, or permission to sit in his presence and cry out to him.

For Lee, those moments were times he retreated to his office or his room to read Scripture and pray or listen to sermons on the internet or songs and prayers on YouTube. For me, it was closing the door to my office and putting on song after song of worship music as loud as the speakers would allow, drowning out the world as I sang and collapsed into the presence of my Savior. It was opening a notebook afterward and watching my hand scrawl ink across the page in words and imagery, painting the colors of my anguished heart onto white-lined paper.

There is beauty in pain.

Just as there is an amazing beauty in the rolling green mountains of central Honduras, there is great beauty in its people. Although suffering is the path of many, their hearts are stout, strong, resilient, and compassionate. Behind their tears is a light deep within that desires to overcome all they face; they are gracious during trials. I experienced this many times, but one day stands out. We hiked hours by foot up into the mountains to survey earthquake-destroyed homes in a remote region in central Honduras and found villagers sitting amid the ruins of their adobe homes cooking what little food they had and then sharing it with us.

Boiled corn and pataste, a green bumpy pear-shaped vegetable that grows wildly on a vine, never tasted so good. I sat in the dirt alongside them, my hands burning as I held the food in a banana leaf while eating it. There were no plates, no silverware, no napkins, nothing we would consider proper on which to serve food to guests. There wasn't even anywhere to wash my hands, but it is forever etched into my mind as one of the best meals I have ever eaten because of the love the villagers demonstrated during their need.

For years I have written in my journals and told stories to groups who have come to join us in this work and to supporters of this ministry when I visited them in the United States. Many times, I have been told I must tell my story, but it isn't my story that needs to be told. This journey God has led me on is more about the people whose lives he has touched. It is about hope and healing and purpose no matter what obstacles present themselves or how many wounds and scars exist. It is about justice, of making things right.

This is a journey for the brokenhearted, to learn to walk in brokenness and how healing and empowerment grow with each step of the journey, when we permit God to use our broken and fractured souls to change ours and others' lives.

Now I must begin to tell their stories—and mine. Let there be more of him and less of me as we begin this journey together. Take my hand as we walk into the darkness with a journal entry, a prose poem, I wrote during an extremely difficult time during 2009 when I felt alone and overwhelmed with the task before me.

—ɔ ⌒

I want to scream and shout because the chaos that exists in this country is out of control. Songs that heal and revive me scream from the surround sound on my desk. They penetrate my soul until nothing exists but the music and the words, a fetus that grows inside me ready to burst forth, the pains growing stronger and stronger, closer and closer until I can no longer breathe, and I push . . .

These last few weeks have been like living in the midst of an ever-growing hurricane. Lives shattered like homes hit by waves beating the shore, whipped by winds of murder, rape, and abuse. Floods of tears inundate us as we try to tread water and bring rescue to victims, all the while preparing to dodge bullets from those who do not want to be exposed.

A man kills his brother and sister-in-law. His father attempts to murder him, his wife and three-year-old child.

A son, age forty-two, rapes his eighty-one-year-old-mother.

A child, twelve, is stolen from her bed at gunpoint and taken to the home of her kidnapper who violently rapes her and later dumps her on a deserted road. Investigators do nothing; they are paid off by the rapist's brother.

A radio and TV personality rapes an eighteen-year-old girl. He harasses her on live television and radio, then walks free because his family threatens the victim to not testify and pays them money.

A single mother of four gives birth to a fifth child and in desperation dumps his five-day-old-body in a septic tank.

A mother sells her ten- and fourteen-year old sons to a man to be his slave labor because she doesn't want the responsibility of caring for them anymore.

A forty-year-old man sexually assaults a nine-year-old girl.

A forty-nine-year-old man takes a thirteen-year-old girl as his wife with the permission of her mother.

A man leaves his wife of nine years and abandons his five children to run off with a new wife, a twelve-year-old girl.

An elderly man is murdered, his body stripped naked and dumped into a river.

A teacher beats an eight-year-old student.

A stepfather beats a thirteen-year-old stepdaughter; her mother runs off with the aggressor while the child seeks help from the police.

These are a few of the headlines in my life—my cases—during these past weeks. Sometimes I wonder if we make any progress . . . Why am I here?

I am the boy with his thumb in the leak in the dam, watching as other leaks sprout. But I don't have enough fingers and some of the leaks are out of reach.

Will my toes work?

I watch as cracks crawl up the cement and teardrops squeeze out under the pressure from behind . . . some leak blood.

I love the song "Jesus in the Dark" by Manning Avenue:

If you felt all that I feel now would it make a difference?
If you've heard all that I've heard would you be free?
Say the word and I'll be there and let love be the reference
If you dare to risk it all and come with me.

Chorus:
Is he longing to be free?
Does he wake up in the park?
Just because you can't see,
He's still Jesus in the dark.

If I told you I was thirsty would you give me water?
If I told you I was breathless would you breathe?
If I told you I was lonely would you even bother?
Would you give up what you have to be with me?

Would you help me if my mother said she didn't want me?
Would you be there if they tore me from the womb?
Would you cry at all or would you feel that this was freedom?
Can the temple of the Lord become a tomb?

I often wonder if people can sense what I feel here. If they heard and saw what confronts me daily, would they believe? Would they even care? If they sat as I did all night with twelve-year-old Nicole and her sister after Nicole's rape, while she bled and bled and bled, waiting for the forensic doctor's office to open at 8 a.m. If they held that child and her grandmother and mother in their arms the next morning as they cried because investigators would not investigate. If they would, as I did, file negligence and corruption reports against the agents, knowing that if anyone found out, a bullet or two or three could have their name on it?

Is there anyone out there who understands this crisis? Does anyone even care? Who can hear the sobs and cries of women and children echoing through the mountains longing to be free from this storm of oppression?

Or are their voices muted like the tree that falls in the forest supposedly without sound because no one is there to hear it?

I am breathless.

Will you breathe for me?

INTRODUCTION

LOVE IN ACTION

If we had known what God planned in sending us to Honduras, we would never have come.

The idea of carrying a gun alongside my Bible, working with presidents and first ladies, as well as other top government leaders, and the thought of changing a nation was beyond anything I could comprehend—in the beginning.

Then there was the danger. Surviving assassination attempts, dealing with rape, child and spousal abuse, kidnapping, murder, sex trafficking, and working in one of the most dangerous places on Earth was definitely . . . *not* on my bucket list.

We had no idea what God planned for our lives. It was too big and terrifying for our minds to believe it was possible. He said go . . . and we went.

Sometimes the Lord grows you into his plan for your life, a little at a time, until suddenly you find yourself someplace you never imagined you would be. His thoughts and ways are higher than ours and any dream or vision we could imagine would never reach the heights, size, or victory of the vision he creates. The vision is always too big and too impossible to realize, which is exactly his plan because we would absolutely know it was the Lord who made it come to pass and not ourselves.

I am titling this book *Journey to Justice*, but that might make it seem as if the journey had finished, when it never will. Life with God, and in his calling, is a constant journey. The vision—or calling—never comes to an end. It grows and continues to change each day.

The story I am about to share with you is one of struggle and faith, of learning and growing—of obedience. It is only a thread; a piece of the masterpiece tapestry the Lord is weaving in our lives and in the lives of the people we meet along this journey.

It is also a journey of discovery, of who we are and who God meant us to be. A story of failures and struggles in the midst of God's handiwork.

Let me quote Pastor Steven Furtick in his book *(Un)qualified*[1]:

"Jesus came to put hands and feet on God's love for broken mankind. Jesus met people in their messes and his whole-hearted acceptance and love changed them forever . . . What God does even through our weaknesses is bigger, better and bolder than we could have asked or thought."

We joke and tell people we work in the dark side of ministry, doing things people would never do, going where people would never go, seeing great wonders and great horrors. But it is the truth. Faith and obedience, serving God is an action. Most Christians will give and pray and some even serve but going into the darkness is not something everyone does . . . nor should they.

Jesus went into the ultimate darkness of hell and the grave for us and rose again giving us everlasting life. He has sent me and Lee into the darkness.

---

1   Steven Furtick, *(Un)Qualified* (Colorado Springs, Colorado: Multnomah Books, 2016).

This is where we live amid rape, corruption, death threats, murder, spousal abuse, sex trafficking, and betrayal. It is amazing and frightening, and we can't do this without him.

Before you begin to believe we are special, let me clear that right up. We never would have taken the first step if we had we known what God planned. Every step along the way we feel unqualified to do this work. But God loves using the unqualified. He calls them, appoints them, and enables his children to walk into the destiny he planned for them.

All we must do is be obedient and say yes, even if we do not know what we are saying yes to.

"For it is God who is working in you, [enabling you] both to will and to act for His good purpose." (Phil. 2:13 NIV)

Ken Wytsma, in his book *Pursuing Justice*[2], writes: "Looking after those who require everything and seem to give nothing in return is the very picture of God's love for us. . . . We are never closer to God than when we are pursuing justice by serving others . . . Justice is rooted in the character of God, established in the creation of God, motivated by the love of God, affirmed in the teachings of Jesus, reflected in the example of Jesus, and carried on today by all who are moved and led by the Spirit . . . Justice is a mosaic. It's not only about single pieces—it's also about all the pieces working together in a stunning whole . . . Justice is rooted in the character of God and flows from the heart of God . . . God's heart beats with justice."

God has called us both to walk in justice ministry. You cannot separate justice from God's love, from ministry, or from faith. Doing justice is God's love in action.

---

2   Ken Wystma, *Pursuing Justice* (W. Publishing, an imprint of Thomas Nelson, 2013).

Author's note:

Because of the danger and threats detailed in this book, I have mostly used only titles and first names of people. In a couple of instances I used a full name, changed a name altogether, or used only a title and letter to identify a person.

SECTION I

HAD WE KNOWN
WHAT HE WOULD DO . . .

CHAPTER ONE

FIRST STEPS

"The LORD said to Abram, 'Go from your country,
your people and your father's household
to the land I will show you.'"
Genesis 12:1 (NIV)

We landed in this tropical land with four suitcases and not a clue as to what we were called to do. Our ministry, Heart of Christ, first began when my husband, Lee, and I came to live permanently in Honduras on June 28, 2005. We didn't know what it was we were supposed to do; we only knew that God called us to be here.

The prior year, in 2004, we came for ten days of ministry in the village of La Ermita and to work with a children's home in Zambrano. As we were beginning to pack up to go home, the other members of our team were talking about how they had a great time but were happy to be going home. I began to feel as though we were leaving our home not returning home.

As departure time neared, a panic began to grow inside me. And as our plane raced down the runway and climbed into the air above Tegucigalpa, the city and mountains sinking from view, tears rolled down my face. I felt as though I would never see home again.

The feeling didn't escape me after our return to Alabama. My husband had no clue of the turmoil inside my spirit, or how my soul ached to be back in Honduras. He hadn't seen my tears on the plane because he had been bumped up to first class, and work, church (he was pastor of two churches), and the children all kept us both busy during our first few days at home.

When we finally had time to debrief and talk about our experience, I shared the feelings stirring deep within me. I told Lee how panicked I had been to leave Honduras and how I sensed an overpowering need to get back there. He told me he had had similar feelings while packing to leave and during our departure, a feeling that had only grown since our return. We prayed. It was then we realized God was telling us to sell our home and cars, quit our jobs, leave everything behind and move to Honduras.

God did not inform us of what he wanted us to do in Honduras. This made it difficult to raise money when people asked what we were going to do there. So, we had to fake it. You can't just tell someone, "God told us to go but he didn't say why." Only an idiot or a fool would say that. Nobody sponsors idiots or fools.

When people asked what our vision was, I would say—with the most confident voice I could muster—"Uhm, we will feed the poor, teach the Good News, help the sick. You know, what all other missionaries do."

The only thing I could give them were Scriptures in Isaiah 58 and Isaiah 61 because every time I prayed for Honduras, the Lord gave me those Scriptures.

". . . to loose the chains of injustice and untie the cords of the yoke, to set the oppressed free . . ." (Isa. 58:6 NIV)

". . . He has sent me to bind up the brokenhearted, to proclaim freedom for the captives and release from darkness for the prisoners . . ." (Isa. 61:1b NIV)

I was able to tell them that when I went into prayer, I felt this darkness, like a cloud hovering over me, slowly descending until it pressed me to the ground. A huge darkness and pain pressed onto my spirit, and when I came out, my face was always wet with tears and I was greatly shaken. It was much later in our journey that the Lord revealed to us what significance that and the Scriptures had in our ministry.

For the moment, we were content to believe he would reveal our purpose in his time.

Our announcement to family and friends yielded varying responses. Some were excited and supported us, a few were angry we did not consult them, and others were brutal. We were told it would be hard to sell our house. We told them if God wanted us to go, it would sell. The house sold within the first week it was on the market—and for asking price.

We were told no one would rent a house or apartment to us to live in for the few months we needed in Alabama to arrange our passage. Everyone would want a year's lease. Again, we told them if God wanted us to go, he would work it out. A few days later a couple from our home church contacted Lee and told him they owned a duplex house and one side was empty.

"You can rent it for however long you'd like," they said.

The battles and challenges to our faith didn't end there. We were told we couldn't raise enough money in the short time we had. But I believe my greatest area of faith was for my daughter Ashley. She was graduating from high school three weeks before we left for the mission field, and I was greatly burdened with how we were going to help her with college. We did not have the money. And of course, some family members had been cruel, telling me I was a horrible mother and was abandoning my daughter by moving away as she entered college.

But God is faithful, and when he tells you to do something, even if you don't know what it is, and you obey, he provides. Just before we left, Ashley received a huge four-year scholarship to a Christian school.

These events during our year of preparation were the founding blocks of our growth in knowing that God would provide for whatever circumstance. It didn't mean we were not nervous—we were. But we kept our eyes fixed on Him and continued walking in obedience.

On June 28, 2005, we arrived in Honduras, landing in the capital city of Tegucigalpa, facing the unknown with a pounding in our hearts, but confident that he would be with us. Several individuals and churches supported us with the funds we needed to get started, and many have stayed with us through the years as monthly supporters. Every cent that comes to our ministry comes from people, churches, and businesses who support the work.

La Ermita, the village our ministry is based in, is near a town called Talanga, the center seat for the county (*municipio*) of Talanga. The main town or city in a county usually has the same name as the county. When we arrived, there were 18,000 residents in the *municipio*, with about 2,500 of them in our village. Today, the county has about 30,000 residents. There is only one paved road in La Ermita. It winds north from the town of Talanga up into the central mountains of Honduras.

Our village, nestled in Talanga Valley eight kilometers from Talanga, is filled with winding dirt roads, pastures, fields of corn and beans, and animals that roam freely as they eat the grass alongside the main road. Animals come into people's yards if they aren't fenced, and we have been in our living room watching television as cows, pigs, horses, and even chickens and turkeys walk up to our front door and look in at us.

We are surrounded by mountaintops at an elevation, I believe, of about 3,500 feet in the *departmento* (state) Francisco Morazán. Homes are built of blocks or adobe, and some with scraps of wood and tin. Many homes have dirt floors and tin roofs. Not all homes have electricity. Those closest to the paved main road are constructed with better building materials while those farther out are more like shacks. It isn't uncommon to find a beautiful home next to a dilapidated one.

My favorite time of day is during the late afternoon when a breeze crawls over the mountaintops on the eastern side of the valley and blows westward. I love to sit on the porch of the dormitory building facing the eastern mountains with a cup of coffee. The winds erase the day's heat and refresh us. Our ministry site is situated on the main road facing east. Across the road is a police post built of adobe with orange ceramic roof tiles, a town meeting hall, the kindergarten, and elementary schools.

When we first arrived, we lived on a farm outside the village. A year later we moved into the village to a lot filled with eucalyptus trees and a small four-room adobe building with no electrical wiring or windows. The open spaces in the walls where windows had been planned, were covered with metal bars. There was no indoor plumbing. There was an outhouse in the yard about forty feet behind the house and a shower in the middle of the yard.

Today, we have five buildings and are building the sixth and seventh, which will finish the compound. We still do not have running water, but at least we have beautifully tiled indoor shower stalls for bucket baths and toilets that flush by dumping a bucket of water into the bowl. All the roofs spill rainwater into a PVC gutter system into barrels and cisterns.

Talanga sits at kilometer 54 on the road from the capital city, Tegucigalpa, that runs north to the *departamento* of Olancho. If you were to throw a dart at the map of Honduras and hit dead center, you wouldn't find the dart far from Talanga. There were no paved roads in Talanga when we arrived, but through the years the main road through town to the park and a few other side roads in the central part of the town have been paved with cement.

Honduras, which is part of the Northern Triangle in Central America, is considered to have the most mountains of all central American countries and the only one without an active volcano. The country is basically the same physical size as Tennessee with a similar population. When we arrived, there were almost six million residents, but now there are more than eight million. The eastern side of Honduras sits on the Atlantic Ocean, western on the Pacific Ocean, and northern coast on the Caribbean. Guatemala borders the country on the northwestern side, El Salvador to the west, and Nicaragua to the south.

Within a couple of weeks of our arrival in Honduras during the rainy season, half of the local police post collapsed. The adobe gave way and the dirt walls crumbled to the ground. We began to sense in the spirit that we needed to repair the police station. But when we spoke with villagers about helping, their response was to not have anything to do with the police because they were corrupt. The villagers talked about the history of death squads and other problems with the police.

They were terrified of the police and wanted nothing to do with them.

As we prayed more and more about the situation, the Lord told us our entire ministry in Honduras would begin with the rebuilding of the police post. It made no sense to us, but this was what God told us to do. We obeyed. We bought supplies and paid men to repair it.

A short time later, while I was in the village inspecting a latrine we had built for a family, my walkie-talkie for communicating with the ministry buzzed. The frightened voice of our caretaker at the farm said the police were at the mission and I needed to come back. I remember pedaling my bike through the village as fast as I could, wondering what I would find. We were still living on the farm at this time.

As I came around the corner and approached the mission, I saw the yard filled with men in blue and black camouflage uniforms, wearing black flack vests and holding semi-automatic weapons. Every building at the farm was shut tight, doors and windows closed, and there wasn't another person to be seen. Everyone was hiding from the group of armed men in the yard.

Carlos, the sergeant from the police post, smiled at me as he swung open our gate, but that didn't reduce the fear pounding in my heart after all the stories I had heard. I leaned my bike against the brick house in which we lived, and Carlos led me to a tall man in uniform with gold leafing on his cap and two gold suns on his shoulders. He stood there with his arms crossed as I came up in front of him. He appeared important and intimidating.

He greeted me and said he was a police colonel, chief of all the police in Francisco Morazán outside of the capital.

"We are aware of your activities," he said as he began to explain why they were there.

I stood, arms crossed, nodding while my mind raced. They knew of our activities? Were they watching us? Is this a good thing? Is this a bad thing? I was frightened. I wasn't used to having a dozen heavily armed men in my yard.

He began to tell me his superiors desired to strengthen the communication and relationships between the community and the police. He wanted us to act as a bridge between the police and the people. When we went to deliver food or medicines, they would go with us, so the people would see them serving.

We were being asked by the government to stand in the gap and teach the police how to serve the people.

He also asked me to begin English classes with his ranking officers, so they would be able to have better communication and relationships with the missionaries in the area. I agreed that we would work together, and they left.

During the following weeks, the colonel visited us at coffee hour (3 p.m.) and sometimes came to dinner. We shared life stories while we talked of God and began to know each other better. How exciting it was to learn this colonel was a Christian! However, it was a bit intimidating to have their weapons on the kitchen table or leaning against the chairs. I finally told them of our custom of putting coats and bags on the master bed when guests arrived. After that, they would enter, drop their semiautomatic weapons and vests on the master bed, keeping their sidearms and radios when they sat at the table. It was rather odd, but humorous, to see their equipment piled on the bed instead of pocketbooks and coats.

I shared my testimony about having been a victim of rape, being a single mother, suffering domestic violence, psychological abuse, and other things throughout my life. I shared that I had worked as a special needs foster care provider, advocated for victims, had experience in investigation as a freelance correspondent for the *Boston Globe* and writer/editor for the *Decatur Daily*—among other experiences—as well as part of my degree including studies of investigation and forensics.

We learned of his life and love for the Lord, prayed together, talked about family and work.

Ministry is all about relationships.

Everything Jesus did in his ministry was focused on relationships with people, showing us how to live in the same manner. In this moment, God was bringing Lee and me into a life-long relationship with another believer in Christ, who also happened to be a police colonel in one of the most dangerous countries in the world.

One morning, a few weeks after we first met the colonel, a police truck showed up at the gate and the sergeant told me the colonel wanted to meet with me right away. I was still in my pajamas, so I gave him a cup of coffee while I got dressed. I worried something was wrong because of how urgent the sergeant appeared to be about this meeting.

The prior weeks had been eye-opening as we rode in the back seat of a police truck (*patrulla*), delivered food, and visited villagers. Whenever we stopped at a home, the villagers' faces reflected their suspicion and fear as they nervously shook our hands, welcomed us into their humble homes, invariably offering us seats in the white plastic chairs ubiquitous to the country. But after a few moments of talking and explaining what we were doing, they began to relax.

Patrullas are double-cabin pickups, some with metal seats down the middle of the truck bed. A couple of villagers had called me during those first weeks concerned I was in trouble. They had been worried when they saw the *patrulla* go by with me in the back seat and thought I had been arrested.

An air of curiosity began to grow among the villagers. And the police, well, they were enjoying themselves. The officers intently watched us interact with the villagers as we shared the Word of God, prayed over them, and offered food or medical assistance. They had only been trained in a military manner, not a manner of service. They began engaging the people themselves. To see a man in uniform—rigid, cold, and rather frightening—begin to smile, play with children, hug elderly women, and sit and talk with villagers was like watching a miracle unfold before our eyes.

One time a captain from headquarters in Talanga was so excited about a mission, he led it himself. The word "mission" as it is used here, relates to an assigned task, or something we had to do. It was hilarious watching police officers tie down a metal bunk bed and mattresses in the back of the *patrulla*. We delivered the beds to a young mother of five—two being newborn twins—who lived in a mud house with a dirt floor. Her children had been sleeping on the floor. The officers were as excited as the young mother while they put the bunk bed together in her tiny house. They sang and played with the children in the dirt yard after they set up the bed inside the house.

But back to the meeting with the colonel. Arriving at the police station was like walking into a second home because I had been visiting the headquarters quite frequently during the past weeks. Every officer greeted me in the *guardia* (reception) with a hug and smile, calling me their sister or *Mami*. I walked through the swinging door, through the courtyard, and up to the second floor where the colonel's office was located. His secretary greeted me and let me inside, asking if I wanted coffee. I declined politely as the colonel waved me toward the couches and gestured for me to sit.

I sat on the small couch in front of his desk while the colonel spoke on the telephone. I began thinking about how the last couple of months had brought me to be sitting in his office. Only God could have orchestrated this. I remember thinking, "Here I am sitting in an office of a colonel in Central America," and wondering what God was going to do next. More than a decade later, it is still clear in my mind.

I did not know then that this was a life-changing moment.

His desk was well ordered and clean, much as one would expect from the military. In Honduras, the police are a lot like the military. Officers lived at the stations, and everyone saluted their superiors. Facing me on the desk was his name plate: Alex Roberto Villanueva Meza. We knew him as Alex. He finished his call, leaned back in his chair and smiled.

Alex told me about the violence in Honduras and the high levels of abuse of vulnerable groups: women, children, elderly, and disabled. The levels of brutality against women and children was alarming. He told me the police were limited in what they were able to do and were not sure about how to tackle the problem. He had been speaking with his superiors and they wanted to know if I could write a program for victims of violence—specifically focused on these vulnerable groups.

Here we were, only a couple of months into living in this country, and I was sitting in the office of a police colonel who was saying that his superiors, including the minister of security—a presidential Cabinet position—wanted to know if I could write a program to help victims of special crimes. The first thing that popped into my head was that I wasn't qualified for the task.

Why were they asking me? Wasn't there some big, professional organization out there that could do this? Someone else who was more qualified?

We sat in silence for a minute. Then, without realizing I had said it, the word "sure" popped out of my mouth. I was just as surprised that I had agreed to do it as he was happy that I had. We were now committed. There was no backing out.

That's how it is with God. He leads you somewhere without telling you what you are going to do, throws you into a situation that is beyond anything you could imagine, and drops an opportunity in your lap. To be honest, I had no clue what I was going to do.

Alex gave me copies of the laws and legal procedures and some information to understand the culture as well as statistics about the enormity of the problem. I later learned that the Honduran government was receiving a lot of international pressure to do something about the high levels of violence against women and children.

Was God going to use us as part of the answer to that need?

If he was, he was going to have to provide a miracle because my Spanish wasn't very good. At that time, I could understand a fair amount and speak a little Spanish.

The year before we moved, I began to study the language by memorizing words and writing them over and over. I chose thirty-five words each week, writing them four times a day and testing myself each Saturday before I moved on to the next group. We also attended a weekly Latin church service on Saturday nights in Decatur, Alabama, to learn to listen to the language, practice it, and to also learn the culture. In addition, I had been privately teaching English to a couple of women from Mexico during our last year in the United States.

But even then, my Spanish was still not adequate to understand the legal language, nor was I fluent enough to write a program in Spanish. There were many reasons why I wasn't qualified or able to do this project.

But God is bigger than any challenge we might face. Day after day, I sat with my English-Spanish dictionary and the law books, sometimes translating each word as I read the laws and procedures. Something began to happen as I continued through this process. I wrote the entire program in English and sat with two police officers, who assisted me with context, and our dictionaries translating the program into Spanish.

Four months later when it was finished, it was as though God had opened the pathways in my brain, making me fluent in the language. Even today I am amazed because I can think in Spanish, and my husband says I dream and speak in my sleep in it. I believe I wrecked a couple of English-Spanish dictionaries during this time, but throughout it, God helped me, and I came out the other end fluent in Spanish.

It was a supernatural thing.

But let's get back to the program. When we speak of special crimes, we are talking about violence against people in vulnerable groups along the lines of the *Law and Order: Special Victims Unit*. The groups included women, children, elderly, disabled. Common crimes they suffer include domestic and family violence, rape, sexual assault, kidnapping, murder, and sex trafficking, but legally include any crime where the victim is a member of a vulnerable group.

Alex said more than half of all women and children in his country suffered some sort of violence, but less than 30 percent of those crimes were ever reported. And of the crimes reported, less than 12 percent made it to the courts, with only a few ending in convictions.

During the following four months (September–December 2005), I studied the laws in Honduras, the legal procedures and culture, and a couple of programs in the United States that were successful. I also considered the issues—what worked in the system, what didn't work, and what was lacking—from the standpoint of a crime victim, which I had been in several instances. I then reconsidered the same questions from the perspective of an advocate for victims whom I had helped through the years.

Each day I prayed and asked God to give me guidance on what I was doing, and through all of this, I began formulating a program. By mid-January 2006, I had completed the program and titled it *Proyecto de Colaboración de Apoyo para Victimas de Violencia y la Niñez*. In English: *Project of Collaboration of Support for Victims of Violence and Children*. I was excited . . . and nervous. It was all printed out and packaged up formally in a binder.

I don't recall if I had taken the bus, called a cab, or rode in the *patrulla* to the police station that day. My mind was filled with how the program wasn't going to be good enough and would not be accepted. That is one of the biggest battles I face: fighting the thoughts of not being good enough. But I had done the best I could, and I was done . . . or so I thought.

God had something enormous planned that I didn't even know about.

Alex was busy when I arrived, but his secretary took me to his office to wait for him and put a cup of coffee on the desk for me to drink while I waited. A few minutes later, Alex came in, sat down at the desk with a smile, and asked me how I was doing. I told him I had completed the project and held it out to him.

I had thought he would look it over, but he took it from my hands and plopped it on the side corner of his desk and leaned forward, smiling. Looking back, I remember his face glowed as if he had a surprise he was about to give to me. But in that moment, I was a bit flustered because I had diligently worked for four months on this difficult project and he wasn't even reviewing it.

Before I share what happened next, I need to share what I heard in a sermon this morning before I began writing this. Pastor Steven Furtick said, "Life's biggest opportunities aren't always obvious."

Lee and I heard the Lord tell us to come to Honduras. No explanation of what we would do. Just, "Go." We obeyed. The police post in our village collapsed in the rains. God said to rebuild it, and that act of obedience would define our entire ministry. It made no sense, but we obeyed. A colonel in the police told us they need us to write a program for victims. I had no clue what to do. God said to do it—or rather he made the word "sure" pop out of my mouth before I could think to say anything else.

All that to bring us to this moment of destiny. I was peeved that the colonel didn't seem to have an interest in reading, or even looking at, the program I spent four months writing. But he was smiling as though he had a secret and was a child about to burst if he didn't share it.

"Aren't you even going to look at it?" I asked him.

I was unaware that the biggest opportunity of my life—of our lives—was about to be offered. This was a destiny moment. Remember, we are American missionaries who had arrived just six months prior, and I was sitting in the office of a police colonel in Honduras. He didn't ask me. What he said next, he said as though it already was done and decided, sealed and settled.

"Yes, but first let me take you downstairs to show you the office we are building for you, because you are now chief of the *Oficina Integral de Atención de Delitos Especiales*"—Office of Attention for Special Crimes. He continued, "There will be two police officers assigned to you."

I was listening to him, but I was not understanding what was going on. "What are you talking about?" I asked.

He said, "Let me say it again, you are now chief of special crimes. We have an office we are building for you and you have two police officers assigned to you."

I was still not understanding. I sat there, probably with a dumb look on my face. None of this was expected. None of this was the obvious outcome.

"What are you talking about?" I asked.

He said, "Let me write it down for you," and he picked up his pen and wrote out on a piece of paper, speaking as he wrote: "*Coordinadora de la Oficina Integral de Atención de Delitos Especiales.*" He handed it to me.

FIRST STEPS | 39

It was a fact, a done deal. It was destiny. Suddenly most everything in my life made sense. Everything I had ever done, and all that had happened in my life, God was using to lead me on the journey to this moment and what would come of it in the future.

We did not go to the government to begin this work in justice. They came to us. That was God. And God didn't tell us what it was that we would do in Honduras before we came. I believe it is because we would have thought it was too big, too difficult, and too scary.

That night as Lee and I discussed the day's events, I remembered the pain in the prayer. I remembered that every time I prayed for Honduras during the year of preparation, a dark cloud—in the spirit realm—would hover and then lower over me, pressing me. It was so painful, it would bring me to tears. All I felt was pain, darkness, and hopelessness.

There it was: our purpose. The pain and suffering, the injustice suffered, the oppression of the vulnerable. God sent us to bind up the brokenhearted, proclaim freedom to captives, release from darkness prisoners, to loose the chains of injustice, and set the oppressed free. Those were the Scriptures in Isaiah 61 that God had given us. It was beginning to make sense.

As we prayed that night, the Lord revealed that the darkness and pain I felt in prayers for Honduras was the pain and suffering the women and children endured. The pressing I felt brought to us the image of Jesus in the Garden of Gethsemane right before he was unjustly arrested, tortured, and put to death.

At that rock he prayed the Father would take the cup from him. As man he could not bear the pain, knowing what lay before him. But then he chose to continue his journey to our salvation—God's ultimate justice of making things right for us. He rose from his place of prayer, and with full knowledge of the suffering he would endure, he walked to the cross.

Not only did the Lord reveal our destiny that night, but he also revealed our name: The Heart of Christ. A heart that feels and sees the suffering in this world, and knowing the sacrifice and pain to do something, is compelled by love to journey into the darkness. It is a heart that cannot "not" act.

He died for us. And soon He would ask us if we were willing to die for Him.

CHAPTER TWO

IF JESUS
DOESN'T SHOW UP

*"The Spirit of the Lord is on me, because the Lord has
anointed me to proclaim good news to the poor. He has sent
me to bind up the brokenhearted, to proclaim freedom for the
captives and release from darkness for the prisoners."*
Isaiah 61:1 (NIV)

God told us our ministry began with rebuilding that collapsed police
post. It was the craziest thing because it didn't make any sense. But it
only required obedience.

In 2004 God told us to sell everything and move to Honduras without
telling us what the mission was, which presented numerous difficulties. But
all it required was obedience and—I admit—a little bit of faking it.

We went, we rebuilt the post, we wrote the program, and then the colonel
announced—without asking us beforehand—that we would be running the
new police department program. We believed the work would be confined to
Talanga, the town and county in which we lived. But once again, God had
something bigger planned. Our work would encompass the entire state of
Francisco Morazán outside of the capital city.

How crazy was that? If anyone had told me in 2004 that I would be chief of special crimes for an entire state in a country in Central America in 2006, I would have laughed in disbelief.

Not possible! Not me! I am not qualified. Nobody would ask me to do such a thing. Not possible!

On February 20, 2006, a ceremony—or rather an inauguration—was held to officially open the office. Generals came from Tegucigalpa and the media were there; it was a big deal. They placed us in the office to attend victims of vulnerable groups and to work this program we wrote.

I suddenly felt like a fish out of water.

Our program focused on the various difficulties the authorities and victims face in Honduras. We addressed the lack of resources for the police such as vehicles, computers, cameras, staff in the office to attend to victims and their needs. Then there was the lack of training. Officers didn't know the laws or procedures in these types of cases, so we trained them. The needs of the victims were great: transportation, medical attention, food, clothing, refuge, aftercare services, and psychological assistance.

The basic function of the office was to have a specialized group of people trained and available to attend to victims throughout the difficult process of reporting the crimes committed against them, and to walk them through the process while meeting their needs along the way. We did it based on the gospel of Jesus Christ, including prayer and spiritual counsel in everything.

Throughout the work, we were teaching and training police officers, investigators, prosecutors, and even judges to serve and how to treat victims of violence. Over time the authorities asked me to teach all over the country.

We also focused on the public to teach and train parents, students, leaders, and others in how to recognize victims of violence and what to do about it, and how to strengthen families and prevent violence in the first place. It was a busy time.

Our reach soon exceeded the borders of the state. God moved us to teach and preach to authorities and leaders, and minister to those who were suffering throughout the entire country.

We held events in schools and churches, with leaders in the different counties, at conferences, and with other missionary organizations. It kept growing. Everywhere we went the people loved and embraced our work. Even the authorities were excited to learn and begin applying what we taught.

The interesting thing about the position we were in and the subjects we were teaching was how easy it was to share the Word of God. The Lord talks a lot about justice in the Bible. We could rescue women and children and tell them that God sent us to rescue them. We could pray with them and with the authorities. We could teach what God says about justice and standing in the gap with leaders, in schools, with parents, and even the authorities.

As the ministry began to grow, supporters would write to me, or ask me directly when I was in the States, "How are putting on a flack vest, carrying a pistol, and going out with police on missions to rescue victims considered missionary work?" They didn't understand because all they saw was us running around with the police, reporting on criminal cases, and sharing stories of women and children who were rescued after a rape, kidnapping, or beating.

"How is that missionary work?" they'd ask. "Missionaries, they preach, they have clinics and schools and children's homes."

At first it was difficult to explain.

"Close your eyes and listen," I would say.

"Imagine you are a six-year-old child, maybe younger or a little older, and at night your uncle or cousin, or even your father, comes into your bed and begins touching you. Maybe he rapes you. There is nothing you can do because you are a child, and the person raping you is someone who has authority over you. They threaten you, tell you that no one will believe you, so you can't say anything. Or maybe you do tell your mother, but then she is punished, or you are blamed for causing trouble. The sexual abuse continues.

"Imagine you are a twelve-year-old girl. Your father has abandoned your home. Your mother takes you out of school to care for the other children while she goes to work in the fields picking coffee or tomatoes. Every day you wash clothes by hand, take care of the babies, and cook all the food—even though there isn't much food in the house. Your mother returns angry and tired. She beats you, insults you, tells you that nothing is ever good enough.

"One day a man in his thirties or forties sees you and comes over to speak with you. Every day he tells you that you are a princess and he promises you a life free from suffering with lots of love. One night you pack your belongings in a plastic bag and slip out the door to run off with him. But his promises were lies. He beats you, rapes you, insults you, and once you discover you are pregnant, he abandons you on your mother's doorstep.

"Imagine you are a fifteen-year-old girl, living in the mountains with your entire family in a small, wooden shack your father built from scraps he bought at the lumber yard. Your grandparents are ill, and the tin blackened roof is caving in. Maybe you eat meat once a week and have eggs twice a week. Your father works in the fields, and your mother, who never went to school, stays home to take care of the children and grandparents. There's no money for medicines or for anything.

"One day two men pass through your village and stop at your house. They tell you and your family about jobs somewhere else and offer to take you to work there. They say you can send money back to your family. You'd be the hero, supporting them all. Grandmother kills the last chicken in the yard and fries it up for a celebration the night before you leave.

"The next day, you pack what few things you own in a small bag and leave with the two men. But their promises of work were not what they said.

They sold you to someone who beats you, drugs you, and sells you to men for sex ten, fifteen, sometimes even twenty times a day. You do what they say, or they beat you. They show you pictures of your little sister, and threaten if you don't do what they demand, they will go get her and make her do it. You can't run away and go home; they know where you live. God forbid your family finds out the truth of what you have been doing. You are ashamed, trapped. There's no way out.

"Maybe you live in a village controlled by gangs. They have come to your family and are ordering *renta* (extortion) because your parents have a small business. Your family can't pay, and, as a warning, they murder your brother. You still can't pay, and they murder your grandmother. Your family closes the business, abandons your home, and you flee to another country only to be detained by immigration and told you will be sent back. Sent back to what? Where will you go?

"Maybe you are a wife. Your husband beats you every night. He forces you to have sex with him and gives you infections because he has sex with other women. There is nothing you can do. He says your mother doesn't love you because she doesn't come around—it's more like she can't be near him or he won't let her come around. He says he is the only one who loves you, and you deserve his beating for whatever excuse he can find: 'You're stupid, you're fat, you're ugly.' He pulls your hair and throws you against the wall, punches you in the stomach, knowing you are pregnant with his child. You can't tell anyone, and he tells you if you leave him he will kill you. Maybe you do tell the police, but they don't help and send you back to your husband. There's no way out.

"There is no way to end the nightmare. There's no hope, no answer, no help, no justice. There's no escape. And if Jesus doesn't show up, if Jesus doesn't send somebody into the darkness, what hope do any of these children of God have?"

We serve in the dark side of ministry. You would not believe the things we deal with, the things we see. If Jesus doesn't go into the darkness . . . you have no idea of the suffering. There's no hope, no help, no rescue. This is it . . . this is all there is.

If Jesus doesn't show up and bring rescue, care, and restoration, the possibility of a life without being beaten and abused and enslaved . . . If Jesus doesn't show up in these moments . . . what hope is there?

The things I have seen I cannot unsee. The things I know I cannot unknow. Our ministry is called Heart of Christ. It is Jesus in the Garden of Gethsemane the night he was arrested. When he was feeling the oppression and suffering of the world so profoundly he was sweating blood. As man he asked the Father, "Take this cup from me." But as God, and knowing what his purpose and mission was, he got up, knowing full well what he was going to suffer . . . and he walked to the cross.

That is the heart of Christ, the heart that can see and feel the suffering of the world. That knows the sacrifice, the danger, the suffering and is compelled to do something about it anyway. Not just talk about it. Not just say, "Oh yeah, there's these people and . . ." or "Maybe they deserve what they got because they made bad decisions . . ." or "They were stupid and shouldn't have believed that" . . . or "It's not my problem."

No, it is knowing the tricks . . . and the deceit . . . and the violence that is done against God's vulnerable children. And how these children do not have any hope in these developing countries. Countries that don't have the money for programs or resources.

In the United States you can call the police, and if they are not at your house in two minutes you can file a complaint. You call, and five police cars show up at your house. You call the police in a country like Honduras, and they might never come.

Many police posts do not have a telephone. Most of them don't have a vehicle. Many officers don't know the procedures. I know it sounds unbelievable, but it is the truth.

There's no hope. There are only a few refuges for victims of violence in the entire country, and they have limited resources, budgets, and staff and are unable to serve the number of people who need service.

We began the work the Lord sent us to do. To bring Good News of freedom to the poor, to heal the brokenhearted, proclaim liberty to the captives, and freedom to the prisoners.

This is mission work. It is some of the greatest of all mission work. Through our work, Jesus shows up in the darkness, rescues those who suffer oppression, cares for them throughout the process, restores them to a life free of violence, and empowers justice.

God gave me Isaiah 59 (NIV) to explain the work.

"No one calls for justice . . ." (v. 4)

"So, justice is far from us, and righteousness does not reach us. We look for light, but all is darkness; for brightness, but we walk in deep shadows. Like the blind we grope along the wall, feeling our way like people without eyes." (v. 9–10)

"We look for justice, but find none; for deliverance, but it is far away." (v. 11b)

"So, justice is driven back, and righteousness stands at a distance; truth has stumbled in the streets, honesty cannot enter. Truth is nowhere to be found, and whoever shuns evil becomes prey." (v. 14–15a)

The suffering and oppression of vulnerable groups in a country with one of the highest murder rates in the world. In a country labeled number one in Latin America for rape. In a country where the United Nations claims that 94–96 percent of crimes against the vulnerable go unpunished. In a country labeled as the murder capital of the world for journalists, human rights advocates, and others. Anyone standing in the gap is at risk of being assassinated.

It is a land where corruption is the operating system, and the hope of justice dies in the heat of violence and cold-hearted corruption. It is a land where those who have the courage to fight for the oppressed are beaten down, murdered, and silenced.

"The Lord looked and was displeased [Spanish version says disgusted] that there was no justice. He saw that there was no one, he was appalled that there was no one to intervene." (v. 15b–16a)

I cannot bear the thought of God being disgusted. It is such a strong word. For me, it invokes the image of someone so displeased with something that they vomit. But his Word says he is disgusted that there was no justice. Our Father in heaven is looking down on all of this, and he sees the injustice; he sees the oppression—and he is disgusted.

Furthermore, he is appalled. The word *appalled* is defined as "to fill or overcome with horror, consternation or fear; dismay." He is appalled to see there is no one to intervene. Where are the people of God to stand in the gap? That is what he is calling us to do.

Christ intervened in our sin and brought justice by paying for our sins—unto death. God is all about justice; it is the second greatest theme in the Bible.

"For I, the Lord, love justice." (Isa. 61:8 NIV)

Justice is about restoring what is broken and righting what is wrong. The Hebrew word for justice is *tzedek*, which is translated as righteousness.

This world is filled with injustice: the child who has been abused, the woman who is beaten by her husband, the girl who is promised a better life and sold into sex trafficking, the single mother without child support, victims who seek help and are either rejected by authorities or victimized again, corruption, and a myriad of other things.

He is calling all of us to "Learn to do right; seek justice. Defend the oppressed. Take up the cause of the fatherless; plead the case for the widow." (Isa. 1:17 NIV)

We are to be like him; pour our lives out for the oppressed. For us, the call started here in Honduras and is now growing throughout the hemisphere. We are to be his flesh, standing in the gap, going into the darkness, and relieving the oppressed. We are to stand in the gap and be the voice for those who are silenced.

But just as it was for Jesus, it is for us. Little did we know the depth of the sacrifice, or the danger that was always roaming about like a roaring lion. But we would soon learn as we continued this journey with him.

CHAPTER THREE

IMPACTING A NATION

"The Lord will guide you always,
he will satisfy your needs in a sun-scorched land and
strengthen your frame. You will be like a well-watered garden,
like a spring whose waters never fail. Your people will rebuild
the ancient ruins and will raise up the age-old foundations;
you will be called Repairer of Broken Walls,
Restorer of streets with Dwellings."
Isaiah 58:11–12 (NIV)

Who would have ever thought we would impact a nation?

Before we began the work, less than a third of special crimes were reported, and few of them made it to court. Convictions were rare. Resources were scarce, and public confidence in the police was lacking due to a history of brutality, corruption, and negligence. Victims would report crimes and not receive help, be told to go away, or become victims again at the hands of the authorities.

We were trying to change this and discovered there were many good police officers, investigators, prosecutors, and judges among the corrupt and negligent. But history kept the people from coming to them for help.

Education, for both citizens and police—of the laws, victims' rights, and proper procedures—was a priority. I was in the police station to advocate for victims and walk them through their cases from start to finish. We also assisted authorities with resources, such as our office, a computer and camera, and helped organize and provide continuation to cases by supervising the work.

I met regularly with the chief of investigators and with the colonel to inform them of progress on the cases and ask for help when we had obstacles. We also met with prosecutors and judges about cases, all with the goal of assuring that victims received justice.

In the past, when a child went missing, little was done. Investigation was passive, not active. For example, a father would report that a man took his twelve-year-old daughter—forcibly, or not—to be his wife or to have sex with her.

"We don't have resources," "We don't have a vehicle," or "We don't have gas," would be the response.

"When you know where she is," they would tell him, "let us know and we will go get her."

Now, however, we could assure investigations were carried out, help authorities with what they lacked, and assist them in interviewing witnesses and persons of interest. We would also go out and look for the missing, which never happens in Honduras.

I am not saying the government authorities were incompetent or all were corrupt. There are a lot of good men and women serving in the police, as investigators, prosecutors, and judges. The main problems are the circumstances in a country like Honduras. Lack of resources and training is the greatest challenge. Corruption and negligence were huge problems, but they weren't the only ones.

In most cases it was the ability to respond and the knowledge of what to do that was lacking. For example, if you have only a few police trucks to cover ten counties and a population of more than half a million people, your ability to respond is limited. How are you going to answer the calls for help? Especially if you don't have gas, or a driver, or the vehicle is in the shop.

We assisted the authorities with these things, and something began to happen. Prior to opening the office, only about a hundred and sixty-five special crimes reports a year were filed in the northern half of our state, the jurisdiction for Talanga police headquarters. During our first eighteen months, we handled more than five hundred reports and then more than six hundred every year after.

I began to receive telephone calls from high-ranking authorities in Tegucigalpa. We regularly worked with and submitted reports to the Supreme Court, Public Ministry (prosecutors), National Police, Center for Human Rights, the child welfare ministry, Ministry of Women, and others. They wanted to know why our region was suddenly such a hotbed of sex crimes, child abuse, and domestic violence.

It wasn't that the violence had increased.

The increase in crime reports did not reflect any increase in violence. It only reflected the growing confidence in the citizens that they would receive help if they reported crimes.

In November 2006 Talanga radio station owner Jose Hernandez asked us to take our message to the airwaves. We began producing a weekly show called *A Life Without Violence*, which focused on strengthening the family, diminishing violence, creating a culture of peace, and other themes along these lines. The program has a listening audience now of more than half a million people.

The news was getting out, as well as the promise of the gospel. The training of authorities, leaders, parents, pastors, churches, and students in the communities was bringing information to the people and giving them confidence that help, and hope, existed. And that we are called by God to stand in the gap.

The success of the ministry grew. National police headquarters in Tegucigalpa began sending me around the country to spread the message. They sent me to places with exotic names such as San Pedro Sula, La Ceiba, Copan, Ocotepeque, and others to train police, prosecutors, investigators, judges, and others in the laws, procedures, and treatment of special crimes victims.

The police frequently move their people around. We worked with many officials and colonels in Talanga as new ones arrived and old ones moved to other posts. Those who had worked with us in Talanga wanted the program in the new areas where they were assigned, because the justice model we were running was working.

I was sent to Olancho during 2009, the largest state in Honduras northeast of Francisco Morazán, to the town of Juticalpa. With the help of their resident police chief, Colonel Palma, we opened an office there with police assigned to work with me. We trained the police in the entire state, appeared on local television and radio to share our vision and God's Word, and worked with the people throughout Olancho.

Another chief of police with whom we had worked, Colonel Mazzony, was assigned to the remote state of Lempira on the western edge of Honduras along the border of El Salvador. He brought us to the capital city, Gracias, and helped us train the police in that state and install another office there, which I also supervised.

I was traveling between Talanga, Juticalpa, and Gracias, supervising the work of the police and the cases they handled covering three states. Every day they would call to report or seek counsel. Once a month I spent a week in Gracias and two days in Juticalpa to review the work and cases, as well as meet with authorities.

The justice work was growing beyond anything we could imagine. At times it was hard to keep up with it all. We kept working and training authorities, rescuing victims, counseling them, helping their cases get to court, and providing for their needs. It was hard to believe that, in a short period of time, I had become chief of special crimes in three states.

Only God could do something like that. Who was I to be doing this work? But here I was, in God's wisdom and strength, every day, walking with him and seeing the impossible happen.

The work was going so well that officials wanted more offices. I told them I was at my limit managing three in different corners of the country. At that point we began training police in Esperanza, Intibuca, Santa Barbara, Ocotepeque, and other places, where they opened offices and managed them on their own.

There was a list of different states where they wanted us to go and train the authorities in our justice model, so they could open their own offices. It was amazing.

During the early years of the work rescuing women and children, we realized there was an enormous lack of shelters nationwide. There was one in Tegucigalpa, *Calidad de Vida* (Quality of Life), and it was struggling to survive, serving only a few victims at a time.

Victims of rape, violence, and abuse, had no place to go if they needed shelter. In all criminal cases in the northern half of our state (ten counties), victims must go to Talanga, where the prosecutor and police investigative unit are located, to file their criminal reports. They are far from home.

One day I clearly realized the need for shelter as I walked from my courtyard office at Talanga's police headquarters to the front lobby. There was a swinging door that police and criminals came through to get to the cells. An abandoned infant was in our care, and a female officer had been assigned to care for the baby. As I approached the swinging door, I noticed the baby sitting on the ground nearby, and the female officer was nowhere to be seen. Suddenly the door swung open, missing the baby by a few inches, and four officers came hustling through with a man in handcuffs.

That moment is forever engraved in my memory.

During the previous months, women and children had come to file reports, give testimony, and have forensic exams by the local doctor. Many times we had to buy food, diapers, bottles, and other things they needed.

I discovered that if their process was incomplete or had been completed late in the day, there were no buses to get them home. Those same women, in the same clothes they wore when raped, or holding babies in cloth diapers leaking on their laps, had to sleep on the wood benches on the front porch of the police station in the cold because they had nowhere to go and no means to buy food, or anything else they needed. Some began walking home even if it might take four to eight hours to get there. Some would try to hitchhike alone with their children on dark roads at night.

One woman, after she left our office just after dark, began walking the long, dirt road to Cantarranas, a village a half hour by truck from Talanga. Along the way men grabbed her, dragged her behind bushes and gang raped her. Someone found her, beaten and bloody on the roadside, and brought her back to the police station for yet another crime report.

We rescued children who were abused by their parents or who had been abandoned, but we had no place to care for them during the investigation, which could take days to complete. They would have to stay in the police station with a female police officer until their cases were resolved. If an infant had been raped, she had to stay in the police station for days while her case was investigated.

I know this is shocking. The truth is the truth, and even if it shocks you—which it should—I am going to tell you the truth about what is going on. It is difficult to explain what it is really like in this place: the poverty, the violence, the corruption, the love, the people. It is unlike anything we could imagine.

Be forewarned, this is not a tidy, pretty story about God's work. It is messy and ugly and beautiful at the same time. This is what real life with the Lord is like. Going into ugly places and bringing his light and love into hopeless situations. It is getting dirty, being tired, loving, and serving when you are beyond your ability to do anything. It is looking the devil in the face and snatching God's children away from him. Alleviating suffering is not pretty. It isn't easy. And sometimes serving God can be dangerous.

Women, children, and babies would have to stay in the police station surrounded by drunks, drug traffickers, abusers, rapists, and murderers the police brought in. They also faced hunger because no one helped them to buy food, and cold as they shivered on the hard benches on the front porch of the police station all night, or if they were children, on the benches or on foam mattresses on the ground in the courtyard beside the jail cells.

In November 2007 we rented a house across the street from the police station and hired a woman to be available when we needed her to care for victims. We gave them food, love, counsel, medicine, and took care of them as long as they needed us. We provided diapers and formula for mothers with babies and paid their bus tickets when they left to be sure they safely arrived home. We took them to the doctor if they needed medical attention. We prayed for them and with them for restoration and justice.

We sat alongside them through this frightening and difficult time in their lives, sometimes holding them all night as they cried. We held their hands when they couldn't say another word, much like Avalon's words in their song "Testify to Love:" *I'll be a witness in the silence when words are not enough.* We went to the forensic doctor and held their hands through the examination. We went with them to court and sat outside the courtroom praying and interceding for them while they testified.

That was the beginning of the shelter—and the physical building of the ministry in La Ermita.

My husband left for the states in 2007 and I stayed behind. Lee went to share the work and solicit donations from supporters to buy the land and build the ministry. Some people told us we couldn't do it. The economy was bad, there were so many world disasters like Katrina, the earthquake in Haiti, and others. So many reasons why it could not be done. But we knew if we obeyed and walked with the Lord, he would provide.

We firmly believed the ministry would be debt free. We wanted to pay cash for the land, the construction of buildings, and for a vehicle. Lee was away for the most part of two years, visiting me for a month or two every three to nine months.

People began to doubt our relationship.

"They must be having problems to be apart so long," they'd say.

But they didn't see what we saw. They didn't have the fire burning inside them for the work we knew God wanted us to accomplish. It was a sacrifice we were willing to make because we knew there was something big on the other side.

We knew it was impossible in our own strength and it still is today, but if this was what God wanted, then he would provide it by moving the hearts of his people to join us in this ministry to the lost and forgotten, the beaten and the bruised.

And he did.

So many loving people and churches joined us in this work, providing money, prayers, and emotional support to make this a reality. Some have come and worked alongside us building buildings, praying with villagers in remote places, and caring for the clients we serve in our refuge and home.

Heart of Christ might be me and Lee here on the ground working alongside Hondurans, but it is also all the people who support this work.

People whose hearts have been moved to be a part of justice, champions who stand by our side through the good days and encourage and pray us through the difficult days.

We bought half of the two-acre piece of land filled with eucalyptus trees in La Ermita where we were living in the four-room adobe house during June 2007. We paid cash for 90 percent of it and agreed to a year of monthly payments for the rest. The owner refused to sell all the land because he thought he might want to do something with the other part in the future. But we knew all of it was ours.

During November 2007, we paid cash for a 2005 Nissan Frontier with a double cabin, four-wheel drive, 3.0 turbo and eighty-thousand kilometers of use. The pickup was black and silver with tinted black windows, which was great for keeping victims hidden inside during missions. A group of children in a Sunday school class in Alabama raised half of the funds for the truck. Other supporters provided the rest.

We broke ground and began constructing the refuge during May 2008. A team came from Alabama to help our Honduran workers with construction. We built a ten-foot wall around our perimeter, with a sliding gate to our parking area. Along the back side of the property we built a one-story dorm building with four bedrooms, two showers, two toilets, a cistern, and a two-room apartment. The four bedrooms we planned to use as refuge bedrooms and the apartment for staff who lived on site. There was a large courtyard in the middle.

The previous year we had built a patio off the back of our adobe house and installed an indoor toilet with septic and an indoor shower. No more runs to an outhouse or showering in the middle of the yard.

Every block, truck of sand, bag of cement, piece of rebar was paid for as we bought it, little by little. Sometimes we spent two months constructing, then a month not, three months constructing, two not. On and on it went.

Until May 2010 the first part of the ministry center was finished and free from debt.

We moved the refuge from the rented space in Talanga to our mission refuge in La Ermita. At any time of day or night, with or without warning, police, investigators, or prosecutors show up at the door with someone who needs our help—short term.

When we first arrived in Honduras, Lee and I decided we would not have a children's home. We were adamant about it. But something we discovered changed our minds. God showed us a need that wasn't being filled. Pastor Michael Todd of Tulsa, Oklahoma, stated in his sermon "Marked" that we need to be the answer to problems. That was what God was doing, making us the answer to problems, filling in the gap where there were needs.

That is one of the ways you know God has marked you for something. He gives you a vision that fills a need. He is the master of filling the voids.

Through our work it was common for us to rescue girls who were pregnant. Some of them ran off with men at the age of twelve, fourteen, or sixteen. But others did not. We encountered girls who were pregnant from rape and incest on a regular basis. Brothers, cousins, uncles—even fathers—sexually abused girls. Mothers sold their daughters to men for sex to feed their family. Some allowed their boyfriends to rape their daughters because if they reported the crime and he went to prison, they would not have money to support their families.

I especially remember our first case like this in early 2006. Neighbors had reported that a ten-year-old girl was pregnant because her mother sold her to men for sex to feed her family. The police arrested the mother, and a man who regularly had been having sex with the child. The ten-year-old sat in my office while her mother and the man were in the jail cells just outside my door.

I remember her sitting on a plastic chair, her dirty and shoeless feet barely able to touch the floor, hands wrapped around her growing belly on her small body. Her face was devoid of emotion, and her voice cold and steady as she described in detail all the men who had sex with her and what they had done. Her mother and the man went to prison, and she went to the government orphanage, which was much like a prison for children.

There were many more cases like this. One during May 2010 changed our ministry forever. Marlen Reyes, the representative of the office for women in the county of Guaimaca, and a good friend who has worked with us since 2006, called. She told me the doctor at the health center had reported that a fourteen-year-old girl had been impregnated by her father.

I spoke with the prosecutor and the investigators, loaned them our vehicle, and off they went. Several hours later they showed up with a woman and eight children, asking us to house them in our refuge for the duration of the investigation. The father was in the jail cell in Talanga.

This case touched our hearts, and after much prayer, we spoke with authorities and received permission from the government to open a home for girls pregnant by rape and incest. This young girl, three months pregnant by her father, was our first daughter. We love all these girls and children as our own and try to give them a family environment. We fill the role of Mami and Papi in their lives and try to teach them what a real God-centered family is like. Through the years we have been blessed with many daughters.

At that time in Honduras, girls who became pregnant from rape and incest, and didn't have family support, were sent to the government orphanage. There was no love or care at the facility. It was just a place to house them. But that changed May 17, 2010, when Heart of Christ Home began receiving such girls who found a home filled with love and care along with our refuge clients.

Between May 2010 and the end of 2013, we continued construction on the facilities with the financial help of supporters and teams who came to help us build. Above the refuge we built a visitors' center with four bedrooms, three toilets and three showers, and a two-room apartment for interns and staff. In the middle of the courtyard we built another building which houses our administration offices, two dorm rooms for guests with a private patio, and our storage room.

God reminded us of the piece of land behind us that the owner didn't want to sell. It was where we wanted to build the girl's home. In 2011 the owner came to us saying he needed money and sold us the piece of land. We paid cash.

During 2014 we began building the girls' school on the backside of the refuge, and during 2015 we began building their home and a playground in front of the school. On Dec. 14, 2017, the children moved out of the refuge and into their ten-bedroom home, which is solar-powered and has cisterns catching rain from the roof that store 60,000 gallons of water. It is a beautiful home, light and airy, painted with beautiful flowers and ferns on the walls. It is a place filled with peace. It is a masterpiece.

The construction of the school and home was paid for with donations from our supporters. For years we were the only home in Honduras specifically for girls who are pregnant by rape and incest. Most homes would not accept girls with their babies: "it was too difficult or complicated" the other missionaries told me. But now, after speaking with other missionaries and sharing this need, we can say we are not the only ones.

The work we were doing was successful. We were working nationwide. We thought we were only coming to work in a village and had no idea about the things God was going to do.

We ended up impacting a nation with this justice ministry. But when God brings miracles and success, the devil doesn't like it. Everything was going well.

Little did we know there would be great battles to be fought, and we would be fighting them soon.

CHAPTER FOUR

GROWING PAINS

"All nations will be blessed through you."
Galatians 3:8 (NIV)

"Opposition arose, however . . ."
Acts 6:9 (NIV)

Growth and impact are painful and messy. Where there is growth, there are growing pains. When something is born, there are labor pains. With impact there is also backlash. Messy things happen when there is backlash. The devil is always roaming about, seeking whom he might devour.

Although the people and many of the authorities loved our work, others did not.

Doing television and radio interviews is a part of life. When men rape children, kidnap girls, sell children as sex slaves, or murder their wives, the media is there to ask what our opinion is on the outcome of the case or how the investigation is going. Sometimes it was like fending off the paparazzi.

Once while I was standing in front of a mass of people with cameras, microphones, and cellphones in my face, one reporter stepped up and asked,

"Why do you hate men so much that you come to this country to put them in jail?" The crowd hushed, watching and waiting for my response.

How do you answer a question like that? I explained I didn't hate men; I had not come to put them in jail. God sent us here to rescue those who were suffering violence and to empower justice in their cases. That reporter was never satisfied and ambushed me every now and again with hateful questions and comments.

In any work that puts you in the public eye, there are misconceptions among the people. Because of this, I gained local status as *La Gringa*.

In the streets people would say men don't beat their wives because *La Gringa* would send them to jail. Parents would tell their children if they didn't behave they would take them to *La Gringa,* who would send them to an orphanage. *La Gringa* is a term for an American woman, but here it usually refers to me. Its origin came from the war between the United States and Mexico. American soldiers wore green uniforms and the Mexicans would shout, "Green go!" The male form of the word is *el gringo*, and the female, *la gringa*.

I never sent anyone to jail. The justice system did. We only empowered the course of justice in the cases we handled. I never sent children to orphanages either. That one really irked me. I didn't like being used as punishment or threats to children.

When I encountered children with their parents in the street and the parents pointed at me and said, "That's her. You misbehave, and she will send you to an orphanage," I would get mad and tell the children I was a defender of women and children and protected them from people who wanted to do them harm. And I chastised the parents for saying that to the children. I didn't want children terrified of me.

But it wasn't only the children who were afraid of me. I remember one time I was at a restaurant and a waitress came up and asked if I was Gracie. I told her I was, and she began to tell me about the night her husband began to get violent with her. She said she held up her cellphone and told him she had my number, and if he hit her, she would call me. I liked and respected that one.

One day when buying blocks for construction, I encountered a situation that clearly demonstrated the minds of the men and the impact our ministry was having on them. It disturbed me because I did not want to be perceived as anyone's enemy. I was here to serve God, not make enemies. But when you serve God, you do make enemies.

I was alone in the pickup and had to drive down a steep, winding, gravel driveway to get down by the river where men were making blocks. As I came around an adobe house, all the men in the yard scattered, disappearing behind a panel truck at the end of the yard by a wooded area at the base of a mountain.

I parked the truck, climbed out, looked around the yard and began to shout, "Is the boss here? I need to buy blocks!"

One by one, faces peeked out from behind the panel truck and finally a skinny man with a shaved head appeared, walking slowly toward me, eyeing me suspiciously. I explained I was there to buy blocks for a building we were constructing, and he began to relax and talk prices, when I would need them, and how many.

Before I made the order I told him I wanted to inspect the blocks to be sure they were of good quality. He pointed to the panel truck, and we walked over to the men standing behind it. They had been loading blocks into the truck to make a delivery when I had arrived.

The first few minutes standing there with them was rather comical. Some of the men were small framed, others large with baggy pants and shirts, but all of them were shuffling nervously, some with their hands in their pockets and their heads hanging low. It was almost as though they all wanted to disappear, like they were afraid of something.

I remember looking at a big, heavy guy with a tattoo and asking him what was wrong. He shuffled his feet, shrugged, then looked at me and said, "We saw your truck coming and when your truck comes, somebody goes to jail." Nervous laughter erupted among the men, but I assured them I was only there to buy blocks.

Another voice came from a small man in the back of the group, "Jose ran for the mountains and he hasn't come back!" I asked him why and he replied, "He has problems with his girlfriend and figured you were coming for him!"

We all laughed and while I was negotiating block prices and discussing delivery dates, I couldn't help but think that something was wrong with this picture. I didn't want men to be so afraid of me that they ran and hid or took to the mountains because I was pulling into the lot. I wasn't their enemy.

It is amazing how the devil can twist something good around and put fear into people that doesn't need to be there. Men feared me; children feared me. That wasn't from God. And I didn't like it.

Then there was the blame. It was my fault men went to prison. It wasn't their fault for having sex with a twelve-year-old girl.

"She wanted it," they'd tell me from the jail cell. "She pursued me!"

The families would blame me too. It didn't matter if the man nearly beat his wife to death, if he had sex with a three-year-old boy, or if he murdered his wife. In everyone's mind it was my fault he was going to prison. I didn't even have to be involved with the case. It was still my fault.

One day I was at the radio station across the street from the police headquarters doing our live show, which aired at noon. From the windows I saw a crowd had gathered in front of the police headquarters. I asked Jose, the owner of the radio station, what was up.

"Two men had sex with a twelve-year-old girl," he said. "They had been drinking all day, and the two guys had sex with her."

I knew nothing about the case because I had taken a couple of days off to rest. I was only in the radio station that day because I had to do the show every week. Once on the air, we began receiving calls about the case. People were blaming me for the men being arrested.

"The girl had seduced them," they said. "She had gone off with them willingly, she got drunk with them and willingly had sex with them both. Why are you ruining their lives?"

I fended off the calls, saying I was on vacation and knew nothing about the case, but they wouldn't listen. It was a mob atmosphere. After the show I had to sneak out of the radio station, jump into my truck and hightail it home before anyone saw me.

The next morning my cellphone rang. It was the mother of one of the men, and she was calling me from Spain. She was asking me to intervene in the case because it was ruining her son's life. I explained to her that, first, I didn't have anything to do with her case, and second, I couldn't do anything because the law stated that anyone who had sex with a child younger than fourteen was committing special rape, which had a sentence of up to twenty years in prison. It was the same as having sex with a four-year-old girl. It didn't matter if the girl involved was a willing participant.

We talked a bit, and then I prayed with her. She was thousands of miles away, and we had never met. Her son was about to be convicted of child rape. But it was a powerful prayer. We prayed for mercy, for truth, and that God would protect her son regardless of what happened that day in court.

After the call I turned on the local news. Talanga's reporters were out in full strength covering what some termed "the travesty of justice" of two men in their early twenties facing conviction for raping a child who wanted to have sex with them. They interviewed family members and neighbors in front of the courthouse, and everyone was saying they were going to drag me by the hair through their village if I ever showed my face.

When did serving God, loving, and rescuing people out of suffering make me public enemy number one? I didn't have anything to do with the case, and yet, it was my fault. I was alone, sitting in my living room, watching a mob threatening me on television. My husband was in the United States raising money for construction of the ministry center and visiting with sponsors, and I had no one to turn to in this moment.

I turned to God, and he reminded me of Peter and Paul and how they suffered beatings and how they were chased out of towns. Even Jesus was so hated that they nailed him to a cross. That was one of the moments when I realized how dangerous and messy it is serving God. The journey for justice, or even just the journey with him, is a perilous one. It isn't safe.

Later I would learn just how hazardous this journey could be.

All of this gives testimony to the ministry's impact. Victims see real hope in their cases, and aggressors see consequences when before there weren't any.

When the political crisis hit during 2009, missionaries and ministries stepped back. Organizations like USAID, Save the Children, Plan Honduras, and others paused their work during the crisis. The Peace Corps left Honduras, and as of this writing, haven't come back. I used to train their members in personal security every year when the new recruits came. I was permitted to teach them; however, their policy forbade their people from working with me because, "it was too dangerous."

One day during the crisis, I was in national police headquarters in Tegucigalpa meeting with the head of the national police gender office. One of the generals I knew walked through and stopped when he saw me.

"What are you doing here?" he asked.

I told him we were working on a project.

"You're still working with us?" he asked.

He explained that all the ministries they were working with had stepped back during this time because they didn't want to be perceived as supporting either side in the crisis. I told him we were still working because there were people who needed our help. Crisis or no crisis, we still had work to do.

"You're the only ones," he said. He hugged me and left.

I was shocked. The country was suffering more violence, and victims had just as much need—if not more. In addition, less help was available for victims because authorities were focusing on keeping the peace during the crisis while their limited resources were stretched even further. We had to keep working.

Also, during the 2009 crisis, people would stop me in the streets and ask when we were leaving.

"Why do you think we are leaving?" I asked them, confused.

"All of the missionaries are leaving," they replied. "We figured you were leaving too."

"This is my home," I told them. "We are not going anywhere because we have no place to go, and there is too much work to do."

Every time I had that conversation with someone, there was a look of panic on their faces while we spoke. I told them we had no place to go. We had sold our house and given away our things to come here. This was our home, and here we would stay. A wave of relief washed over their faces, and it was as though our presence meant there was hope.

These encounters made me realize that even though we were struggling with the idea and the real threat of people hating us for this work, the ministry had an impact on the people in this nation because we stayed during the crisis. I believe that our leaving, if we had decided to do that, would have snuffed out any hope the people had.

Through much prayer during this time, with the revelations we were having regarding image and perception, we developed a strategy to change the negative image of the ministry and what we were doing. We began a campaign on our radio show and spoke about courageous men of God. We were looking for the brave and valiant men we knew were here. Men who would stand up to protect women and children and join us in this fight for justice. When I drove down the street I kept my windows down and waved at the men as I passed them, with a smile on my face.

Over time things began to change—at least with the perspective that I was against men. My cellphone would ring late at night, calls from men helping women in villages and seeking my help and counsel.

One night a man in a village in the mountains had rescued a woman whose husband had beaten her and was hunting her. The man wanted to know what to do because the police couldn't come until the morning. I told him how proud I was of him, and that God was pleased to see him being a courageous man of God. I advised him to lock the doors, shut off the lights, and keep silent watch through the night so her husband would not find her in his house. And I told him I would be praying.

Another night while I was still at the police station late handling a rape case, my cellphone rang. A man told me a man in his village had just shot a teen boy and they needed help. I ran to the colonel's office, and he dispatched a *patrulla*. The boy's life was saved, and the man who shot him was arrested.

The next morning I called the man back and asked him why he called me.

"You were here last month teaching us all how to rescue victims," he said. "We didn't have a number for the police, but we had your flier with your phone number on it."

Among the general population the perspective changed, and men began to step up. However, it was a different matter among the families and friends of people who had committed crimes against women and children. They loved us and our work until their brother, or husband, or son was in the jailcell. Then, in their minds, we became their enemy.

As I explained earlier, when we began this work, only about 30 percent or fewer of special crimes were reported, and convictions were rare. Because we added resources and training, counseling and supervision, and advocated for victims, we were able to increase the number of reports (*denuncias*) to an estimated 90 percent.

This success was because the people finally believed that justice would be served. And it was. Some 70 percent of the reported cases ended in court convictions or acquittals. All this in a country labeled by the United Nations as the most violent country in the world with a 94-96 percent impunity rate.

During 2010 we had the only conviction in the country for sex trafficking. Officers we had trained recognized that when a young girl was on the street at 1 a.m. with two men, they should stop and investigate. What they discovered was a horrible case of two men who promised a family a job for their twelve-year-old daughter. She would go with them around the country selling clothes, and she could send them money. The parents gave their young daughter to these two strangers. Instead of selling clothes, they sold her to men for sex and were on the verge of selling her to international sex traffickers when the police came upon them.

I vividly remember her day in court. She was terrified. I told her that when she went in to give her testimony I would be praying for her without stopping until she came back out. I told her not to look at the men and to just look at the judge or the prosecutor and feel the presence of Jesus in the room as though he were standing behind her with his hands on her shoulder.

"You are not alone," I told her. "He will be there with you."

The judge's secretary loaned me her office where I could pray when they took Heidi into the court room. I began interceding on her behalf, eyes closed, praying out loud, pacing the room. About ten minutes later the court door opened, the prosecutor and secretary came out with Heidi, who was trembling and crying.

"She can't do it," the prosecutor said. "She can't testify."

I put my hands on her shoulders and pulled her close to my face, looking into her tearful brown eyes.

"You saw me praying here," I told her. "This is your moment, all the power is in your hands, all you have to do is tell the judge what happened. Those men can't hurt you. You did nothing wrong. You have no shame for what happened . . . they do."

"If I pray over you again," I asked her, "would you be able to go back in there and testify?"

She nodded and sniffled as she wiped the tears from her face with the bottom edge of her blouse and blew her nose into it. I hugged her and began to pray. I prayed God would give her courage to tell her story. I prayed that Jesus himself would show up in the court room to be her protector and witness.

As I was praying, I heard other voices and felt movement around us. When I finished and opened my eyes, I saw that the prosecutor, the judge's secretary, and another woman had laid hands on her and prayed with us.

"Jesus will be right there with you," I said as I hugged her.

Heidi walked off with the prosecutor, who had her arm around her like a mother hen protecting her chicks under her wing. The door to the court room closed.

I began to pray again. It was some time before the door opened and they came out. This time, Heidi had a smile on her face.

"I did it Mami Gracie. I told them everything, and I felt Jesus right there with me."

"I am so proud of you," I said as I pulled her into my arms. "You are the bravest girl I know."

Through the years that we had the offices in the three states; we trained more than forty-five thousand parents, children, students, and community leaders. We also trained more than four thousand police, investigators, prosecutors, judges, and other authorities. We handled more than six thousand special crimes cases with a 70-71 percent closure rate.

Nothing like this had ever happened in Honduras before. It was a huge victory.

However, with great success also comes great danger.

SECTION II

MIRACLES
IN THE MADNESS . . .

CHAPTER FIVE

YOU WANT ME TO GO WHERE?

"Go into all the world and preach the Gospel to all creation . . .And these signs will accompany those who believe: In my name they will drive out demons; they will speak in new tongues; they will pick up snakes with their hands; and when they drink deadly poison, it will not hurt them at all; they will place their hands on sick people, and they will get well.' "
Mark 16:15-18 (NIV)

Danger comes in many forms when you live and work in one of the most violent places on Earth. Each time I left the ministry, Lee prayed I would come home alive. I will never forget the morning in July 2008 when two of my friends were murdered, or what happened ten days later.

It was early, the sun was barely up, and the air was filled with fog. We had just loaded a group of more than twenty missionaries into three vehicles with two police officers and were leaving Talanga to drive six hours or so to San Pedro Sula for their return to the United States. My father, nephew, and son were flying in on the same airplane the group was flying out on to Atlanta.

We had to drive to San Pedro Sula, a city in the northwestern part of the country, because a plane had run off the runway in Tegucigalpa, closing the airport for several months. I have driven to San Pedro Sula many times, but this time it was the longest and most painful drive of my life.

I was driving the first vehicle of our caravan as we left Talanga, when one of my police officers in the second car called me.

"Do you have the radio on?" he asked.

I told him I hadn't been listening to the news because we were having a conversation.

"Turn on Radio Talanga," he said. "Something horrible has happened."

I can still clearly hear his voice and remember a sense of dread fill me, like whispering dark fog fingers curling around my heart. I asked the missionaries to be quiet and turned on the radio as we approached the exit for the road to Tegucigalpa.

I listened to Jose Hernandez on his morning news show tell the story of what happened in El Guantillo, a small, remote village nestled in the mountains about ninety minutes north of Talanga.

The previous morning shots rang out at a cantina in El Guantillo. The three police officers on the other side of the village in their post were told they were needed at the cantina because someone was out of control and might hurt somebody.

The officers ran through the main dirt road of the village and encountered a man who had been drinking all night. The man was armed and had been shooting into the air in his drunken state. They took him into custody and began the long walk back to the post, guiding the man, who stumbled because he was drunk and restrained by handcuffs.

The main road of the village is tucked in a valley with the mountains rising on each side; modest adobe or block houses scatter the hillsides. The village is known to be filled with *mojados*–men who had gone to the United States illegally, worked, and brought money back or had been deported back. It was also known as a village in which drug traffickers lived.

About halfway through the village, new shots pierced the morning silence. Word had spread through the village that this man was in police custody and some of his friends in the houses on the hillside above the road began shooting at the officers. What ensued was a massacre as men, armed with AK-47s and other automatic weapons, chased down the officers. Two were shot dead in the middle of the street in the dirt, and one escaped. After murdering the two officers, the men stood over them and emptied their weapons into the bodies, making them unrecognizable.

The third officer who escaped hid inside the trunk of a tree in the mountains surrounding the village for many hours because he had no cellphone signal to call for help. It was later that day, during the afternoon, when the National Police and Cobras (SWAT) forces entered with more than a battalion of officers to bring home the fallen men and rescue the one hiding from the villagers who had been hunting him for hours.

The villagers threatened that if any police returned, they would kill them. They said if police came back to the post, which they had shot up, or ate anything in the village, they would die because the villagers promised they would poison the officers' food.

The two officers who were murdered had been close to us. The younger of the two, Murillo, had been a close friend of my son, who was flying into San Pedro Sula that afternoon. He was always praying with victims and had helped take care of a missionary team the previous year. He loved the Lord. While he had been a police officer for a couple of years, he looked like a teenaged boy. He was thin and small framed and kept his hair styled to attract young ladies. His laughter came from deep within.

The other officer, Sergeant Hernandez, was a close friend of ours. When he had been assigned in La Ermita, he passed many evenings eating dinner with us. He had thick, black hair, parted to the side and a small moustache. He was full of questions about the Lord and why we did what we did. He was the epitome of curiosity. And he was gentle spirited—you could see it in his eyes.

I remember the night Sergeant Hernandez received Christ Jesus as his Savior at our dinner table. We had been talking about ministry and the Lord. A moment presented itself when Hernandez was talking about how dangerous his job was as a police officer, and we shared the plan of salvation with him. He decided to make Jesus his Lord, and as we sat down to pray together, the power went out. We were suddenly plunged into darkness.

Lee grabbed a few candles and lit them, placing them on the dinner table. We joined hands, and Hernandez prayed and received the Lord into his heart. I clearly recall his face in the candlelight as he prayed. It was full of peace and hope. The moment we said amen, the power came back on. We laughed about the drama of the power going out as we prayed and coming on as we said amen, not knowing that a few months later he would be transferred to El Guantillo and die such a horrible death.

I listened to Jose Hernandez recount the story over the radio and interview police officials and civilians as my hands clenched the steering wheel and our caravan continued its journey first south, toward the capital city of Tegucigalpa, then north on our way to San Pedro Sula in the northern part of Honduras.

In that moment nothing existed except the voice on the radio and the road in front of me. As our caravan rolled down the roads, the mountains, trees, and valleys passed in a blur. The quiet conversations of the missionaries in the truck murmured on, but my mind was somewhere else.

A hand slid gently onto my shoulder from the back, and I heard a voice break through the veil of pain tightly holding me.

"Are you alright?" a missionary asked.

The gesture brought a wave of emotion I had to push down. I couldn't let it out. I had to be strong. I was the leader, and we had a long journey ahead of us. I shook my head and wiped the tears off my cheek with the cuff of my black sweatshirt, trying with all my power to keep the emotions from overwhelming me.

I remember wondering: How I was going to have the strength to get through this day? How was I going to be able to drive six or so hours without falling apart? And then drive back another six hours with my officers, father, son, and nephew? What was I going to say to my son, who loved these two men? Tears cascaded down my face, and I continued to drive, focusing on the road ahead, praying for strength.

Just after we passed through Tegucigalpa and were on the road north toward San Pedro Sula, I had no more strength and I pulled to the side of the road, looked in my rearview mirror and saw the other two vehicles pull up behind me. I turned off the engine, shoved open the door, and ran over to the side of the road and let the dam burst.

I crouched down in a ditch on the side of the road and violently sobbed and cried until nothing more came out. Officers Sanchez and Chavarria had run over to me, as did the missionaries. It was a dark moment for me. I felt as though I had been swallowed up by darkness. It had sucked me down to the very bottom. I couldn't breathe; I couldn't talk.

I don't know how long we were there. But I do remember hearing prayers and feeling hands over my body. Then it came—warmth began to flow over me, and it was as though the darkness lifted ever so slightly, and peace, cool as an afternoon breeze when a storm approaches, fell over me.

When I was able to speak, I told the group what had happened. I watched as the reality of life in the field spread over their faces. Some expressed disgust over what happened and how; others' faces were blank as tears streamed down their faces.

I looked at my watch and realized we needed to get moving or we would miss their flight. We held hands and prayed again. I asked God for the peace and the strength to be able to drive and get this team on the plane and to receive my father, nephew, and son and drive back. I asked for wisdom in how—and when—to break the news to my son.

I don't remember anything more about the remaining four-hours' drive to San Pedro Sula. I don't remember saying goodbye to the group or receiving the others. My first memory is loading luggage into my pickup and my son standing beside me. Should I wait until we arrived home to tell him? I realized I needed to tell him then because he would notice something wasn't right with me.

"Dominic," I said as I pulled him away from the others and into a hug, "I need to tell you something." I held onto him tight. "Yesterday Officer Murillo and Sargent Hernandez were murdered." He was devastated to hear the news. I briefly explained what had happened, and we took a few moments to share our grief in the airport parking lot as storm clouds rolled in.

It rained the entire drive home, slowing our progress, as though heaven was shedding tears I could not; God's tears falling furiously from the sky. It was three in the morning the next day when we finally arrived at the mission and were able to climb into bed and go to sleep. I was done with this day; there was "no more me." I was empty. I prayed, closed my eyes, and allowed the darkness of sweet sleep to engulf me.

A week later Colonel Antonio called me into his office. Every day we had meetings to discuss cases, plan investigations and other things, so it wasn't unusual for him to summon me. What was unusual was his behavior when I entered his office and sat on the couch in front of him. Usually he was bubbly and liked to joke around—although, at times, he could be very serious. That day he was serious, but also hesitant.

"I need you to do something for me," he said. "I need you to go to El Guantillo."

There it was: the word, the place that had been haunting me for days. Each time I closed my eyes I saw my friends running for their lives only to be shot down in the street like dogs.

I asked the colonel what it was he wanted me to do there, and he said he wanted us to preach on building a culture of peace. I told him it was a hot and dangerous place to be. He assured me he would provide enough police protection to keep us safe.

I reminded him that the people were still saying they would kill any police who went there. They said they would poison any food the police ate, and I wasn't sure police protection was going to keep me safe. He continued to press me and persuade me to go because he believed we were the only hope he had of bringing peace to this village. I continued to back down and give reasons why I couldn't until finally I told him I would pray over it and get back to him the next day.

And I did pray.

There are times in life when God asks us to do something so terrifying we doubt he actually wants it. I prayed, and I prayed, and he told me to go to El Guantillo and preach the Good News; preach unity and peace; preach forgiveness. I argued with God all night.

"Go," he whispered.

The Holy Spirit would not let me rest in peace until I finally agreed. We would later learn that only God was capable of fixing this mess and of bringing peace to a war zone.

A couple days prior, Lee had left for the United States to speak in churches and meet with sponsors. My father had left with him, but my son and nephew, both sixteen, were still with me. I knew I could not take the boys with me on such a dangerous mission, but I also didn't like the idea of leaving the two of them alone for two days. We were going to El Guantillo two days in a row, leaving Talanga each morning around five in the morning to allow us to arrive there by seven, and we had to leave by three in the afternoon each day to get home before dark.

It wasn't safe for us to stay overnight in the police post (*posta*) in El Guantillo.

During the next two days as we prepared for our trip to El Guantillo, the Holy Spirit began whispering to me.

"Take the boys with you."

It was bad enough I was going, but to also take the boys? The day before leaving on the mission to El Guantillo, as the boys were folding fliers, I asked them if they wanted to go, hoping they would say no because they might think it was boring. Instead they both were excited and said yes. I told them I would pray about it and decide in the morning.

As I drank my coffee in the early morning darkness, I prayed and asked God if he truly wanted me to go and if he really wanted me to take the boys. There was no whisper—nothing. But there was peace. I felt peace, cool as the morning air seeping in the windows and quiet as the mountains in the predawn hours. For the first time, thinking about El Guantillo, I sensed only peace.

I woke the boys and told them to get ready to leave. Before you scream at me for endangering the boys know this: there is no safer place than being obedient in the perfect will of God.

It was still dark when we left the police station in Talanga for the almost two-hour drive to El Guantillo. My son, Dominic, and my nephew, Kristian, were in the back seat with an officer. There were twelve of us in all. Nine officers were assigned to keep us safe. Seven of them sat in the truck bed (*paila*) with their bulletproof vests and semiautomatic weapons (Galil ARMs). Two officers rode inside the cab with me and the boys.

The sun began to rise when we left the pavement near El Porvenir, a village 35 kilometers north of Talanga, and began the journey into the mountains on a bumpy, dirt road. It was already hot. There was nothing except the dirt road spitting up dust behind us and the trees.

I kept watching the trees as I drove, waiting at any moment to hear gunfire, waiting for something to jump out at us, for a truck to be blocking our path. But there was nothing. Just the quiet of the mountains. Occasionally we would pass a dirt hut with a tin roof and naked babies could be seen playing in the dust. Women washed clothes in the rivers we crossed.

I hadn't told my son or nephew this was the place our friends had been murdered ten days before. They laughed and joked with the officers as though they were on a great adventure. I didn't feel like it was an adventure. My fingers gripped the steering wheel so tight my knuckles were white. My semiautomatic pistol was on the seat under my right thigh, and the bulletproof vest I wore made me sweat in the heat. I kept praying, watching the woods and the road, as I cautiously drove the treacherous mountains roads.

We topped a hill, and as we began to descend, Official Lobo, the commanding officer sitting next to me, pointed at the village below.

"That's El Guantillo," Lobo said.

It looked like any other village in Honduras. A main, dirt road through the center, with houses crowded around it, others spattered across the hillside above. He then pointed to the side road that led to the *cantina* where the police had arrested the man that awful day. The village housed a little more than a thousand people.

Nothing happens in these villages without everyone knowing about it. As we entered the village, everyone came out of their houses and stores to look at us. I smiled and waved. They stared back at me. At one point the officer at my side pointed ahead to where Hernandez and Murillo were murdered. I couldn't breathe as we drove over the spot where their bodies had lain.

When we reached the other end of town, we found the *posta*, a white-washed adobe building with roof tiles and hundreds of bullet holes on its front. One of the officers pulled out keys, unlocked the door, and pushed it open. We went inside. It was 6:30 a.m. and we had an hour and a half before we had to be at the school, which was located at the entrance to the town—on the other side.

Official Lobo, who oversaw the group, told us to rest in the bunk room for a bit, and he went off to do something. I remember being on one of the lumpy bunks looking at the ceiling and praying. I was on such a high level of alert that every muscle in my body ached from being tense. I closed my eyes and continued to pray.

I don't know how to describe it, but I "saw" us walking down the road through town from the *posta* to the school. I saw myself walking in front without my bulletproof vest and without my pistol. I saw my boys at my side and the police walking behind me. It played over and over in my head, and again I felt peace.

Official Lobo came in to tell us we needed to get ready to go. I stood up, handed him my pistol, and took off my vest. I told him we were going to walk through town, not drive through town. He argued with me, refused to take my gun, ordered me to put my vest back on, and said he was responsible for protecting us.

"We are walking and that is it," I told him, standing my ground. "I am not wearing my vest or pistol. They outnumber us with people and weapons. The nine of you can't keep us safe. Only God can prevent a massacre in this dark place.

"How can I talk to people in this village about peace and unity while wearing a vest and carrying a gun?" I continued, "That promotes the image of being afraid of them. We have to leave the truck here and walk."

He didn't like it, but since I had the keys to the truck and was determined to walk, he agreed. But he did remind me that it was breaking protocol, and if something went bad, the colonel would know I refused to follow protocol. He ordered everyone to gather their things and get ready to go.

If you can, imagine this sight. You are in the middle of Central America, in a jungle, in the mountains, in a village on what we would call Main Street—a dirt road—and there is a white woman walking down the road, with two white boys beside her, and nine heavily armed police behind them. Each house we passed, the people came out and either stood in the doors or came to their wooden gates or barbed-wire fences to watch us pass by.

I smiled at each person, said hello, and called out blessings to them. They stared at me, and some hesitantly waved back. If you were there, you would think I was completely at ease, but I was terrified. I prayed as we walked.

The boys beside me were clueless to the significance of what was happening. The officers behind them, well I can only imagine what was going on in their minds as they recalled what happened to their comrades on this very street ten days earlier.

Official Lobo came up beside me, touched my elbow and nodded ahead.

"That's where they died," he said.

Emotion flooded me, and I began to tremble as we reached the spot where my friends died. All I could think of was that I must be crazy standing in this village in such a vulnerable state. I stopped on the spot and looked down at the dirt, trying to see if there was any sign of what had happened, but there was none. A minute or two passed as I stood there in silence, tears filling my eyes, flowing down, anointing the ground where they died.

I looked up and saw the villagers watching me; nobody said a word.

"Walk" the Lord whispered.

We continued walking toward the school at the other end of town.

Official Lobo led us to a small house across the street from the school and said a woman there had offered to cook us breakfast. We sat on plastic white chairs in her yard while she prepared our plates. I looked at Lobo in panic, and he assured me the woman had guaranteed the food's safety. The other officers didn't look too confident as the plates, filled with eggs, beans, sausage and tortillas, were placed in their hands.

I don't believe anyone wanted to eat the food—except the boys because they didn't know we were in a dangerous place where the people threatened to poison the food they gave us.

Asking them all to bow their heads, I told them we would pray. I thanked the Lord for bringing us safely to this place, for allowing us to walk safely through the town, and for providing us with food. I prayed Mark 16:18 where it says if you should drink anything deadly it would not harm you, and added that I was believing this included *eating* anything deadly, which drew sideways glances from some of the officers. When I said amen, the boys dug in to their food, but the officers were either looking pensively at me or at their plates.

"Let's eat!" I told them as I lifted my fork, silently prayed Mark 16:18 again and ate the food.

We didn't get sick, nor did any of us die from the food or coffee offered to us.

For the next four hours we spent our time in the classrooms in the school with the teachers and children in grades one through six. We discussed violence and prevention, child abuse, sexual abuse, and all the other themes covered in our teachings in schools.

When noon came, we sat in the school's director's office as more food, sodas, and coffee were brought to us. Again the officers and I were nervous, and again I prayed Mark 16:18. We ate, drank, were filled, and did not die. After eating lunch I saw the courtyard of the school begin to fill with parents and villagers. There was no large auditorium to hold events or meetings. They were held outside under the shade of the trees.

Some villagers brought plastic chairs, others sat on blankets on the ground or on large rocks throughout the yard. This was the big meeting the colonel had asked us to do. Two hundred and forty-six villagers were sitting in the shade of the trees in the courtyard of the school, all watching us as we prepared to speak. They were also eyeing the heavily armed police officers scattered about the courtyard and by the gate.

As I watched them watching us, I wondered what they were thinking. I knew several members of the community had also died in the shootout with the police. The air was heavy with grief, rage, and distrust. It was so heavy you could almost feel the pain in the humid summer air.

The director of the school introduced us to the villagers. There was no sound system, no stage, no microphone. After presenting us she told me it was all mine and stepped aside. I asked the crowd to stand and opened with a prayer.

If I told you I had prepared what I was going to say, I would be a liar. I really had no idea what God wanted me to say. I had a few notes, a few Scriptures, and my Bible. But something occurred as I stood praying over the crowd of broken villagers and police. I felt the Spirit fall hard on me.

After asking the people to sit, I began to speak to them. I can't recall everything I said, but I talked about God's desire for us to live in peace and unity. I told stories from the Bible. I talked about my pain at knowing two close friends of mine had died here and that I knew some of their loved ones had died here too. I talked about the power of forgiveness and how God can heal shattered hearts and broken people.

Tears rolled from my eyes as I spoke, pain poured out in my words. I told them we shared this pain and God wanted to heal us. I talked about justice, God's love of justice and desire to heal broken hearts. I told them God wanted them to live in peace with each other, and with the police. I told them God loved us so much that he sent his son Jesus to die for us. For two hours and forty minutes I preached, and no one left. They were riveted, listening to every word.

Looking back on this now, remembering that day, I can feel the fear and pain. My heart is beating faster. But I also remember the wonder, the awesome wonder of the power of God falling on us all. Half of them had tears in their eyes. Men were crying and so were the police.

When I felt the spirit lift and say it was done, I asked them a question.

"Have any of you ever had a police officer pray over you?"

Faces displayed disgust as heads shook and voices said no.

"Well that changes today," I said.

I asked my two officers who worked with me to each take a turn and pray over the people, the police, and this village for healing, peace, and unity. Officer Sanchez prayed for more than twenty minutes and Officer Chavarria prayed almost as long. They prayed with power and passion. I prayed in the Spirit the entire time.

When the amen was said, nobody's face was devoid of tear stains. An amazing thing happened. As we were cleaning up and the people were leaving, everyone was shaking hands, and many were hugging the police officers before they went out the gate.

It was the first time any police prayed over these people. It was the first time these people hugged and accepted the police. And God moved on every heart that was there. As we walked back to the *posta*, people were smiling and waving at us, not just me smiling and waving at them.

We returned the next day to do classes in the seventh and eighth grades and to speak with the people again in the afternoon. While we were eating lunch in the director's office, a woman came in with a thermos of coffee for me. She wasn't on the list of who was approved to safely give us food.

She told me that when I spoke the day before and was getting tired, I had commented on how much I loved coffee and needed some to help me get through the day. She had brought that gift to me because she was blessed by what I had preached the day before and wanted to be sure I was able to preach again. I thanked and hugged her, and she left.

The officers didn't want me to drink the coffee. I confess I did pause for a moment as I looked down into the plastic cup in my hand. But then I smiled at them, held up the cup, thanked God, and said, "Mark 16:18!" and drank it down.

While preaching to a smaller crowd the second afternoon, another woman came up and brought me a thermos of coffee, saying the same as the woman earlier. I thanked her, told the crowd I was so blessed that two women had brought me coffee, poured a cup, held it up and drank it in front of everyone. All the while, silently praying Mark 16:18.

The power of God moved in that village. During a crisis we were asked to go into a war zone and preach the Good News of the gospel. I admit it was terrifying, but the surrender and obedience to God in the midst of being terrified worked healing, brought peace, restored hope, and worked a miracle.

Three months later a new crew of police moved back into the police post, and they have been there ever since.

Maybe six months or so later, while on our way from Talanga to Tegucigalpa, we stopped at Promdeca, the police post at the entrance to the capital, to use the bathrooms. One of the officers told me they had been stopping the El Guantillo bus to search the men for drugs and guns since the shootout months before. He said that one guy on the bus asked him if he knew *La Gringa* from Talanga. The officer told him he did.

"*La Gringa* came to speak in our village," he said. "I didn't go. But after hearing what she had to say, if she came back, I would go listen to what she has to say."

Many people saw the power of God and were healed from profound pain. My heart was also healed.

"After the Lord Jesus had spoken to them, he was taken up into heaven and he sat at the right hand of God. Then the disciples went out and preached everywhere, and the Lord worked with them and confirmed his word by the signs that accompanied it." (Mark 16:19–20 NIV)

CHAPTER SIX

DEATH IS A DAILY AFFAIR

"Since we have been justified through faith,
we have peace with God through our Lord Jesus Christ,
through whom we have gained access by faith
into this grace in which we now stand."
Romans 5:1–2 (NIV)

"It's only death; it happens," they tell me. "You just get used to it."

I never realized that coming to the mission field and living in a developing country would bring me face-to-face with death on a regular basis. But when you think about the endemic poverty and the lack of medical care, it makes sense. Then there's the violence.

It all started with the dogs. There were four puppies on the mission grounds at the farm when we arrived. I love dogs. To me, they're almost human. Within our first few months of arriving in this land, two died from some mysterious disease. Well, mysterious to us.

The first died violently in front of us, convulsing. I remember my daughter Ashley holding one of the puppies in her hand trying to feed it with an eye dropper because it wouldn't eat. She kept it in a cardboard box near her bed to watch over it during the night. The next morning it was gone from its box. We later found it under a bush, stiff with rigor.

Our Honduran helper, Rosa, said the puppies died from a virus or infection that comes with the rainy season. We've lost several dogs to the same disease through the years.

We were torn up about it, and in her desire to help, Rosa had her children dispose of the bodies for us. We later found out they threw the puppies' bodies over the fence for the vultures to finish them off. A few more of our dogs escaped the yard and were killed in the street by cars. It was hard to deal with the constant loss of a loved companion.

Then people began to die around us in Honduras. Lots of people.

Let me backtrack here a minute. Throughout my life in the United States, before coming to Honduras, I knew only a few people who had died. My paternal grandfather's wife, Grandma Helen, died the night of my Junior prom. I remember Dad waking me up the next morning to tell me. That was my first encounter with death. It affected me for days, including a few days later when I went for my driver's license test.

We all mark death by the events around it. Someone dies at Christmas or Easter, or some other important day and it affects us for the rest of our lives when that day comes around again.

My maternal grandmother's husband, Papa Al, died during my early years of adulthood. I was close to Papa and his departure deeply affected me. My paternal grandmother's husband, Papa Eddie, died a couple of years later, and again the sorrow. My daughter's grandfather passed after suffering from cancer. Rev. Guinn, a pastor from my youth, who was like a surrogate father to me, passed, my paternal grandmother passed, then my maternal grandmother passed.

Eight people close to me died in ten years. Most of them were elderly, so it wasn't out of the ordinary for most Americans.

But then I came to Honduras. I've been here for more than a decade and I've lost count of how many people have died. It's not that their lives didn't matter; it's that I can't list them all. It's the quantity that causes one to lose count. I should have known it would be a regular occurrence because our first ten-day visit to Honduras in July 2004 was an indicator of what was to come.

We were heading back to the mission in Zambrano after visiting the Valley of Angeles for our shopping the day before we returned to the U.S. As we rounded the last mountain road curve in the dark, we saw a group of people standing around a body in the road. We pulled our vehicles to the side of the road and went to help. That's the standard American reaction.

On the side of the road lay a man, his body twisted, and his mangled bicycle a few feet away. The vehicle that hit him never stopped. All around him were Hondurans staring at him, smoking cigarettes, talking, observing, but no one was doing anything to help the man.

I remember kneeling next to him and bending over to put my face close to his. His eyes stared right at me as I heard our leader praying over him. I didn't know any Spanish, but I talked to him anyway, telling him he wasn't alone, he'd be alright, we'd get him help.

An ambulance passing with a patient stopped, and I heard a police officer tell the ambulance the man was dead.

"He's not dead!" I screamed. "Take him to the hospital!"

But the ambulance left. I returned to the man's side and stroked his bloody forehead. A few minutes later, as I was nose-to-nose with him, talking to him, I heard a breath escape from his mouth and he was gone.

We returned to the United States the next day, forever affected by what we saw that last night on that dark, mountain road, but never imagining as we prepared to permanently live in Honduras that this event was a foreshadowing of things to come.

A year later we moved to Honduras and so began our dance with death. I cannot count the amount of times I have been covered with blood from attending to victims of vehicle accidents who have died in the street or how many people we served who died.

There was the two-year-old, hydrocephalic baby we tried to save with medical help and food, who died in the hospital in Tegucigalpa after I rode in an ambulance to get him help. And Arthur, with whom we prayed the prayer of salvation one night as he lay on his bed in his adobe shack, and who died twelve hours later.

Don Rufino, who worked for us for a year, I saw hit by a truck in front of our house at dawn, his body parts strewn all over the street. The ten-year-old girl who knocked on our door every Saturday selling pineapple turnovers her mother made was also hit by a car. She died saving her six-year-old sister's life, pushing her into the ditch at the side of the road as the vehicle sped toward them.

There was the woman in the mountains in Marale, whom we found lying in a bed in her hot and stuffy adobe house, windows closed, her body wrapped in some sort of leaves. The green, moist leaves were pasted to her body, wrapped around her legs and waist. To this day I do not know what kind of leaves they were. We tried to get her medical help, but she died before we could get her to a doctor.

We watched our eighty-year-old neighbor suffer for months for lack of medical help. Basically the hospital sent her home to die. And she did. Colonel Antonio's father died suddenly. The doctor gave him medicine for his heart, not knowing the man was an alcoholic. The mixture of meds and alcohol killed him the first day.

Our neighbor, a boy who had spina bifida, died a few months after we got him a real wheelchair. He originally had a plastic chair with bicycle tires mounted to its side. (Hondurans are so creative!) Then there was the elderly grandmother with hepatitis A for whom we dug an outhouse, so she and her family would have a place to do their business other than the yard. She died two months later. The elderly widow who lived in a plank shack behind us was found dead in her rickety shack one morning.

Police officer Gonzales spent a week with us doing events in elementary and high schools in Cantarranas, a village of about three thousand a half hour east of Talanga. Two months later he died in a motorcycle accident, two weeks after the birth of his first child. Officer Cruz joked with me in my office one Wednesday afternoon. Friday morning at 6 a.m. he died in a car wreck.

It would take an entire book to count the lives whose paths crossed ours on this journey and then passed to be with the Lord. But it was one thing to deal with natural death. It has become another to deal with violent deaths. I don't know many people who personally know one person who has been murdered.

Our relationship with violent deaths began on Christmas Eve 2007. A police officer whom we knew at the Promdeca police post at the entrance of Tegucigalpa was shot in the head twice that night. He wasn't a close friend, just someone we talked to and joked with whenever we stopped at that post. In fact, I had spoken with him about thirty-six hours before he died.

It was then that I began counting. During the following twenty-six months, thirty-two friends—police, prosecutors, judges, investigators, human rights advocates—were murdered. It was then that I stopped counting. How do you deal with one, never mind thirty-two?

The next brush with violent death came six months later on June 28, 2008, when Sergeant Hernandez and Officer Murillo were assassinated in El Guantillo.

In the end of September 2008, I met an inspector in Olancho during the inauguration of our victims office. The next morning he went with a group of police into the mountains to execute arrest warrants and they were ambushed. His headless body was later found. They never found his head.

During October and November 2008, two investigative agents I knew in Olancho were murdered in the streets. On May 10, 2009, as I sat with Colonel Antonio working on reports, a call came in that two officers I knew from Olancho were among a group of police chasing down murder suspects, who were ambushed and killed by AK-47 fire.

I saw a notice in the paper about Captain Bustillo, who had worked with me for a year when we first started the victims program. On August 31, 2009, he, his wife and children had been kidnapped by armed men. The wife and children were released, but Captain Bustillo was found executed a few hours later.

On October 18, 2009, another friend, Agent Banegas, was shot dead in Cantarranas. We had been joking and talking on the phone just a couple days before. A week or so later, on October 29, 2009, an inspector and another police officer from Santa Rosa, Copan were kidnapped at gunpoint on a road and executed. I had been with them two weeks earlier when our car broke down in Copan, a remote state on Honduras' western border with Guatemala. The inspector had taken care of us while we were in Copan, and the officer had rescued us from the side of the road.

Then there are the cases we handle. In one year I experienced the heartbreak of four murdered women in Lempira, four murdered newborns in Talanga, two murdered women in Talanga, three murdered women in Olancho, and six murdered children in all the offices.

I'll never forget reviewing and printing photos of two murdered children in Guaimaca during June 2007. Their bodies had been chopped up by machetes and the twelve-year-old girl had been gang raped before her violent death. Or seeing the photos and videos of the newborn baby in Talanga a mother had dumped by the side of a river, alive and connected to its placenta.

Street dogs had eaten the baby alive. Each time I drive by that spot I still see the baby's body on the ground.

I'm still searching for the answer that will help me deal with this much death: natural, or violent.

I was chatting with Colonel Juarez one day, just shooting the breeze and the subject of death came up. I asked him how he deals with knowing and working with so many people who not only die but die violently. He sat back and sighed.

"You just learn to get used to it."

I told him, for me, with people I know briefly or casually it's a sense of sadness and a rock in the chest. The tears don't come. But with those I had been close to, it used to incapacitate me for an entire day. Tears come and go, come and go, but never come with the force to get it all out. Such frequency takes a toll on you, a numbness crawls into your soul.

Death becomes a new normal.

It is urgent to share the love of God with everyone we meet. I remember speaking with a captain in the national police headquarters in Tegucigalpa, who worked in the anti-gang unit. During the late 2000s gangs were bad; today they're your worst nightmare. He gave me a ride to the exit of Tegucigalpa and waited with me for a bus home. This was before we had our pickup.

We discussed the danger of his life and work, and I asked him if he knew the Lord. He said he knew about God and that Christ had died for his sins, but he wasn't ready to receive him.

"I need to clean up my life first," he said. "And I don't think I am ready to do that yet."

I tried to explain that God wanted him just as he was, but he wouldn't listen.

Many officers and villagers have received Christ with us. Others already knew the Lord when we met them. Some we encounter refuse to accept him thinking they will lose out on the fun parts of their lives. But in this place where death and violence permeate our lives, I can only have peace because of Christ.

Being surrounded by so much death has prompted an urgency in me to share the gospel. One minute someone is here, and the next they are gone. I find that if we live our life for Christ and our testimony is not only what we say but also what we do, people will see Christ in us and that opens the door to share the gospel.

I don't cry much anymore when a person I know passes. If they knew the Lord, I have peace and celebrate. If I don't know if they knew the Lord, then I rest in the hope they met him during their life's journey. For those I know who refused the Lord, there is a deep sadness within my soul. And when that sadness is weighing upon me and it begins to rain, I think, maybe the angels are crying for me.

"It's only death. It happens," they say. "You just get used to it."

I don't know that I will ever get used to death, but I do have hope. The hope of his calling, that death is just another step in the journey—a passing from this world into the presence of the Father.

"We also glory in our sufferings, because we know that suffering produces perseverance; perseverance, character; and character, hope." (Rom. 5:3–4 NIV)

CHAPTER SEVEN

EVIL ABOUNDS BECAUSE GOOD MEN DO NOTHING

*"If anyone sins because they do not speak up
when they hear a public charge to testify
regarding something they have seen or learned about,
they will be held responsible."*
Leviticus 5:1 (NIV)

"The only thing necessary for the triumph of evil is for good men to do nothing." I've always admired this quote from Edmund Burke. It has stuck with me for my entire life and has also caused me to get into a lot of trouble. I've always been the person who roots for the underdog, and who defends the weak. And I learned there are consequences—both good and bad.

When I was much younger and worked in an office as a bookkeeper for a nonprofit foster care and adoption agency, I discovered two women were embezzling money. They had taken out credit cards in the name of the agency and were enjoying extravagant lunches and buying gas on the cards. When the bills came in, they grabbed them from the mailbox before our superiors did. I learned about it because I was the accounts payable manager and began receiving calls for bills I could not find.

One day I went to the mailbox while the girls were out for lunch and found these bills, but later that day while I was at lunch, the girls stole the bills from my desk. I had no evidence when I went to the president to tell him. For weeks the women had been harassing me because I caught them sitting around at work on a Saturday doing nothing and billing the agency for overtime pay. I had also begun asking them about the bills. Because of the weeks of complaints about their harassment and the lack of evidence on my part, he wrote off my accusation as personal issues between me and the women.

They found out about my ratting on them and made my life and job miserable for months. I was pregnant with my first child and when I went on maternity leave, the bosses found out that the charges I made were real. The women were fired; I received a promotion. It was worth the suffering to do what was right, though at the time of the harassment, I regretted it.

A few years later I had yet another choice to do (or not do) what was right. I was working as a foster care provider for the state of Massachusetts and had a case where the social workers were endangering the children in their care.

I had a secret meeting with my congressional representative to solicit an investigation into the agency. Six months into the investigation, the social workers discovered I had reported them and made my life miserable. They executed surprise inspections, declared my house—which they had previously rated fine—as unsuitable for foster children, and of course, filed fake child abuse reports against me.

The stakes were higher this time. I almost lost my own daughter, son, and nephew for whom I was caring. But it all worked out. The investigation determined that not only were the children in my care being put at risk by the agency, but other children also were suffering. The agency was closed, the social workers were fired, and I received a letter from the social services commissioner apologizing for the harassment and declaring me free and innocent of the fake charges against me.

That's when I retired from foster care. I couldn't do it anymore.

Fast-forward another few years, and I was working as a freelance reporter for various newspapers. I stumbled across a story about government and public officials using their positions of authority and confidence to convince elderly women who had no family, or were alienated from them, to sign over powers of attorney, which the officials used to steal millions of dollars during a thirty-year period.

I also uncovered potential evidence that they might have murdered three of the five women. An editor at the *Boston Globe* was interested in the story. I was working as a freelance nation correspondent covering various stories for them at the time and began investigating the allegations.

While investigating, someone broke into my house to search my files, someone cut the tubing to my gas tank on my car to make the gas leak out and maybe explode while I was driving. I received threats and even took my children and went into hiding on the advice of a retired FBI agent with whom I was consulting on the case.

The Alabama Attorney General's office found out about my investigation in this case and emailed me while I was hiding out in the mountains of Virginia with my children. They asked me to come back to Alabama and meet with them. The children and I returned to our home and met with a special agent from the Attorney General's office. They reviewed the evidence I had uncovered. We worked together for three years with the agreement that I had the exclusive if I held the story until the suspects went to trial.

I wrote a book about this story, but never had it published. Two of the people involved were arrested and went to court. After the Attorney General's prosecutor presented their case and turned it over to the defense, the judge threw it out, even with all the damning evidence. The prosecutor was furious. He said the judge was up for reelection and all the powerful people who could get him reelected were sitting behind the defendants that day.

That was my first face-to-face with corruption.

The *Boston Globe* didn't publish my story because the case was dismissed. I didn't finish the last two chapters of the book because I was disgusted, and justice fell by the wayside. However, I may go back to the book and tell that story sometime soon.

I now find myself more than a decade later in Honduras, facing horrendous cases of murder, rape, sex trafficking, and abuse. I encounter corruption around every corner, in the police, in the investigators, in the prosecutor's office, and even judges. Victims and witnesses are paid off by friends or family of the guilty party to not testify or pursue the case.

For 500 *lempiras* ($25), *sicarios* (assassins) will gun down anyone they get a contract on. Daily, in television and radio interviews, speaking engagements, and on my radio show, I am telling people not to be afraid and to stand up for justice and testify.

Then I had a case during January 2009 of a twelve-year-old girl named Nicole, who was taken from her house at 9:30 p.m. at gunpoint by her stepfather's boss who had been in their home watching soccer with the family. He took her to his house where he violently raped her.

The family called the police because they discovered the child was missing and presumed the man had taken her. When the police arrived at his locked and dark house, he held the gun to her head and put his hand over her mouth to silence her. She told us she could hear the police outside looking for her, but they went away. The man dumped her on a dirt road at 1 a.m. and she found her way home, and then to the police.

The DNIC (national department of criminal investigation) in Talanga called me at 3 a.m. to take care of her that night in our refuge in front of the police station until she could see the forensic doctor at 8 a.m. This was a year before we built the refuge in La Ermita.

During the night I learned that her alleged attacker had a visa or residency in the United States. We also learned he had a white Tacoma vehicle. I called the DNIC agent in charge of the case to ask him to alert Interpol and Honduras' Migration department, so the suspect couldn't leave the country. I also asked him to put out a national alert on the vehicle, a white Tacoma.

He told me he wouldn't call Interpol or Migration.

"Nobody can buy an airplane ticket the same day," he said.

I informed him that if someone has a United States visa or residency, money to pay for the ticket, and there was a seat on the plane, they could buy the ticket and be gone on the earliest flight. He laughed at me.

I pressed him about the alert on the vehicle, and again he refused.

"We don't have the *placa* (plate number)," he said.

"The police do *operativos* and stop vehicles in the streets every day all over the country," I said. "We know his name, so they can stop all white Tacomas and check IDs of the people inside."

Again, he laughed at me and refused, saying it was impossible.

Later that morning as the witnesses and family arrived to give their declarations, I told the agent they were waiting for him, and I went to the forensic exam with Nicole. The doctor made us sit for almost six hours in the sweltering heat while he attended his personal patients. It didn't matter to him that this twelve-year-old child had been raped and had been waiting for this exam—in the same clothes, without bathing or washing—since three in the morning.

It was after two in the afternoon when we returned to police headquarters. The family members were upset and informed me the police hadn't gone to the suspect's house for the crime scene inspection. They said that friends who had passed his house on the bus saw that his family had put a "For Sale" sign out front and were removing everything from the house. They also told me that nobody had taken their witness declarations.

I turned and saw the agent standing on the curb outside police headquarters chatting on his cellphone. I walked over and stood in front of him, with my arms crossed, staring at him until he finished his call.

"Why haven't you gone to the crime scene to collect evidence?" I asked him.

"We don't have a vehicle," he said.

I pointed over his shoulder behind him at my truck.

"My truck has been sitting here since three in the morning," I said. "You know you could have used that."

He shrugged and tried to walk away from me, but I followed and continued talking to him, asking why no one had interviewed the witnesses. His answer was no one was available, and the witnesses would have to come back another day. He opened the door to the investigative offices, stepped in, and shut it in my face.

I called Colonel Antonio and told him about the negligence. Fifteen minutes later an angry investigative agent—a different one—came out of the investigative offices and asked me where the witnesses were. It was after three in the afternoon, twelve hours after the rape victim, her family, and most of the witnesses had been brought to the police station.

To make a long story short, the investigator abandoned the case, never called Migration or Interpol, never put out the car alert, never followed up on any leads, and I had a lot of leads, all of which I gave him and his boss and his boss's boss. The suspect's family cleaned out all the evidence from the crime scene. Nobody did anything to stop them.

I kept pushing the case, talking to superiors to pressure them to do their job. However, there was always an excuse. I couldn't figure out why there was no action on this case. The head of the prosecutor's office and the chief of police ordered action by the investigators. But there was none.

I received information that the family of the suspect were "untouchables." They had money, power, and influence and didn't think twice about ordering a hit or paying off someone. I also received information that the investigator in charge of the case had been paid to do nothing.

Then strange things began to happen.

One day as I returned home after a long day's work, my housekeeper, Sinthia, who lived next door, came running down my driveway. She said that earlier in the day, when she was cleaning, two men were in the wooded lot on the south side of our property at our chain-link fence (before our twelve- to fourteen-foot block walls were built) calling our two rottweilers toward them. Duquessa, our female dog, ferociously barked at them and would not go near the fence. Colonel, our male dog, was jumping up on the fence. But when the men saw Sinthia watching them, they left.

A couple of days later I returned late in the evening and found Colonel dead in the yard. The officers from the police post in front of our ministry came over to help me with the body. They told me the dog had been poisoned.

The next day Sinthia called me while I was in Talanga. On her way home from buying something at the *pulperia* (a corner store), she found a vehicle sitting in our driveway. No one got in or got out. The engine was running, and the windows were blackened, so she could not see who was inside. She crossed the road, walked straight to my front door and, as she unlocked it, she looked at them. She said she had stared at them for about a minute and then the car pulled out of the driveway.

I spoke with Colonel Antonio about these and other events. He expressed concern, saying it sounded like someone had been casing my house for its weaknesses. He said he was sure they were trying to poison the dogs when they were seen in the side lot, and he was confident they had succeeded in killing my dog Colonel a couple of days later. He ordered the officers in the post in front of the ministry to be on alert and ordered me not to go anywhere by myself for a while.

A few days later I was in a late meeting with the colonel, planning for the execution of an arrest warrant for the sexual abuse of a minor. It was too dangerous for me to go on the mission in a remote mountain area, and the police were going to borrow our truck. The colonel drove me to the ministry in La Ermita to drop me off and bring the truck back to headquarters.

As we crossed the small, cement bridge entering La Ermita, the colonel's cellphone rang. He began yelling and telling the officers to call headquarters and radio the police trucks on patrol to look for the vehicle. When he finished the call, he told me someone had planned to kidnap me. We drove directly to the post to get the details.

The sergeant in the post reported that he and the other officer had been eating supper and watching the television news when they saw a van parked on the road in front of my house. Because they didn't want to dirty their uniforms while eating, they had taken off their shirts and only had on their white T-shirts. In the time it took to put their uniform shirts on and get out on the road, the van had left.

He said that about a half hour later, as it was getting dark, they noticed the van parked there again and were able to get out there to find out what was going on. As they approached the van from behind, they saw a man in his twenties knocking on my front door.

An older man, about forty, was in the driver's seat, and a woman was sitting in the seat behind the driver. The van's sliding door on the passenger side was open. One officer stayed at the back of the vehicle to note the license plate while the other cautiously approached the driver.

The officer said the older man startled when he appeared at the window to ask what they were doing. The man told him they were looking for me. The officer informed him I didn't receive people—or cases—at my house.

He told the man I was at police headquarters and that was where he needed to speak with me. He said the man appeared nervous, and when he looked over his shoulder toward my house, the officer also looked in that direction. The younger man, who had been knocking at my door, entered the van and quickly shut the door. The officer then asked for their identification and vehicle registration.

Without warning the van sped off, leaving the officers standing there surprised in the middle of the road with dust in their faces. It was then they called the colonel. I recall a van passed us as we were entering the village when the colonel's cellphone rang. A review of the registration of the vehicle revealed that the owner lived in Tegucigalpa, in Colonia Chile, which is known to be a dangerous gang-ruled neighborhood at the north entrance to the capital. Colonia Chile and its neighboring *colonia*, Cerro Grande, are hot areas for kidnappings.

The *patrullas* never encountered the vehicle. The people in the vehicle never came to the police headquarters asking for help.

Colonel Antonio was confident that these people were trying to kidnap me. He said if they were asking for help for a case, they would have spoken more to the police and left their information, taken my telephone number to call me, or have gone to headquarters to see me. Because they took off when the sergeant asked for their identification, it was confirmation to him.

He believed, or surmised, their plan was to knock on my door, presenting a case or question to me, using the older woman in the van as bait to get me to leave the house and walk to the road where the van was parked. Once I was at the open door of the van, they would grab me and be off.

I told him I didn't believe anyone would kidnap me as we had no money to pay for ransom. I realized then how stupid my remark was. There wasn't going to be a ransom. This was connected to all the other things that had been happening.

Antonio explained that if they had achieved their goal in grabbing me, nobody would have ever seen me again. This was an attempt to assassinate me because of my pushing on this case. He ordered the officers to walk me across the street to my house, to check it and the fence, and to assure I was safe inside. Then he turned to me and told me I was not allowed to leave my house until my officers arrived in my pickup the next day. He said to keep my pistol and cellphone close by, and to call him if anything happened.

He wanted to assign an officer to stay inside the house with me for a couple of days, but after the last time a year before, I wouldn't let him. Fortunately I was leaving for the United States three days later to meet up with my husband and attend Ashley's graduation from Martin Methodist college in Tennessee.

Nothing ever happened with the case. A year later the alleged rapist returned from the United States and was living in his house, which had not sold. We were able to get an arrest warrant, and he was arrested. However, when the victim and the witnesses were called into headquarters after his arrest, they timidly said it wasn't him—it was somebody else.

It was him. They had identified him by name, by his house, his profession—he was her father's boss. They even identified him by a photo from a party. But suddenly he was back, and the victim and witnesses said it was someone else, and they didn't know who.

We would have had evidence from her clothes if, on the night of the rape, the investigator did what I told him to do. It was a hot night, heavy with humidity, much like a summer night in southern Alabama. At three in the morning when I received Nicole, they had a plastic bag with her underwear and other items in it. I told him to preserve the evidence in a paper bag or something that wouldn't kill the evidence in the heat.

The following afternoon, while we were at the forensic doctor's office waiting to be evaluated, the investigator showed up with the same plastic bag in hundred-degree heat. I knew then the evidence was lost. We had nothing, and now the witnesses were recanting the suspect's identity.

When I filed corruption and negligence reports against the investigators, I had the opportunity to speak with the internal affairs agent handling the case. She told me phone records revealed the investigative agent had been speaking with the suspect all night long on his cellphone—and several times the next day. She also informed me that the man accused of raping the girl was a known drug trafficker who had residency in the United States.

When I think about that case, I remember holding Nicole all night long in our temporary refuge as blood ran down her legs. I remember praying over her and rocking her in my arms through the night. I remember praying with her family on the front steps of the police headquarters and in their home when I visited them there.

This is what gospel justice is all about. It is about helping those who are suffering oppression and walking with them through the darkness. Praying with them through the danger. It is about standing up to monsters, regardless of the cost.

You can say that all was lost. Nothing ever happened to the rapist. He went free. The family was threatened and paid off. Even the investigator who handled the case got off. He was never charged or punished for throwing this case, destroying evidence, or conspiring with the enemy. But God showed his power in that he had angels camped around me, protecting me from harm as I did his work.

Evil abounds because good men do nothing . . . and, sometimes, even when good men or women do something and stand up for justice. But that is not the end of the story; it is not the end of the journey. We keep fighting the good fight of faith, we keep running the race. And, yes, many times justice does win.

CHAPTER EIGHT

LOVE CALLED HER NAME

*"It was for freedom that Christ has set us free.
Stand firm, then, and do not let yourselves
be burdened again by a yoke of slavery."*
Galatians 5:1 (NIV)

He carved his name in her back twice with a machete to assure no other man would have her. Her name is Gloria and I encountered her one day, hiding in a shack made of adobe with a dirt floor. She was afraid to open the door to let us in because she believed that if she spoke to us her husband would kill her. She had reason to believe his threats. She said he had killed three people and made her clean the knife and burn his clothes after one of the murders.

I learned about Gloria's case when her sister entered our office seeking help. Gloria and her fifteen-year-old daughter had gone into hiding because they could no longer take the abuse. For eighteen years Gloria suffered torture, abuse, and terror. Her daughter had been sexually abused by her own father.

Gloria's sister told us he had threatened to kill the entire family, a common act in this country, if they didn't make her come back to him. More than five thousand women have been murdered in Honduras between 2005 and 2016. In many instances, children and other family members have also been murdered.

"He keeps coming to our home," she said. "He busts in the door, screams at us, and demands we tell him where she is. He searches the house and threatens to kill us if we don't tell him where she is or bring her back to him. We are terrified."

She sat in my office sobbing as she grabbed the bottom of her blouse and used it to wipe her tears and blow her nose.

"He won't kill you," I tried to assure her. "These men use lots of threats to manipulate women and their families to do what they want."

Her eyes were a cold fire.

"He's already murdered someone," she said. "He will kill us."

She told us her sister and niece ran away a month prior and that he had been bothering and threatening them the entire time. I asked if she knew where her sister was, and she told me she was the only person who knew and would take us to her.

We gathered a team of investigators and police for the rescue mission. They loaded up with bullet-proof vests and weapons and piled into an old, red pickup owned by one of the investigators. The one vehicle their department had was on another mission. Wilfredo, the owner of the vehicle and head investigator, asked if I could help with gas. He didn't earn enough money to pay for gas for missions in his personal vehicle, and his office wouldn't approve a reimbursement for gas for his truck. We had a budget to help victims, and it included gas to rescue them.

The officers climbed into the pickup bed. Wilfredo, Gloria's sister, and I were crammed in the tiny cab. We drove for two hours until we arrived at a tiny, adobe shack, perched on a hill, far from her home and our office. The yard was filled with dirt and chickens. The sun beat down on the closed shack, its tin roof glistened in the heat.

Wilfredo had to pound on the wooden door several times, its watered-down white paint peeled and stuck to his fist. There was no answer. We turned to Gloria's sister, who was still sitting in the pickup and asked her if she was sure this was the right house. She said it was.

He continued to pound on the door as the other officers took up positions around the shack until we heard a voice from inside tell us to go away. He pleaded with her to open the door, told her that her sister brought us, that she was safe, and we were there to help her. There was no response.

A few neighbors began gathering along the edges of the property and the dirt road in front of the house, curiously watching us. Officers moved them back as I went up to the door and spoke to her, telling her who I was and about our ministry. I heard movement inside the shack.

The door cracked open and all I could see in the darkness were her terrified eyes staring at me. Her face was barely visible. We spoke softly for what seemed like forever as the sun rose high in the sky and sweat poured down the back of my neck. She didn't want to let us in and you could hear terror in her voice.

I remember feeling frustrated and helpless. I begged her to open the door and let us help her, but she refused, saying over and over, "He will kill me." Closing my eyes, I prayed for God to help. I didn't know what to do.

"Gloria, look behind me," I said. "Look at all the help here. There are police here to protect you and your daughter. Trust me. Let us in."

A small voice came from behind her. "Let them in Mami." It was her daughter, who had been hiding behind her mother in the dark, hot house. Our eyes locked for a moment and then Gloria slowly opened the door a bit and stepped back, letting us in.

The adobe shack was as common as beans in Honduras. Its uneven dirt floor was rutted where streams of water ran through during rain storms. There was a bed made of wood with a thin piece of cushion over a piece of plywood, the sheets dirty from much use by an unwashed body because she was too afraid to go outside to wash them, or herself, lest someone see her and inform her husband of her whereabouts.

In the corner was a wooden chair that leaned to the right on the uneven floor. A musty, moldy smell assailed my nostrils, and the only light in the room came from a small, glassless window that she cracked open as we entered, letting in flies and mosquitoes. A few spots of light hit the floor where sunshine peeked through holes in the tin roof. In the corner was her bathroom: a bucket and a pail of water.

Gloria hobbled over to the bed on her uneven handmade crutches, and sat. Her face was weary from worry and fear, her voice soft and reticent. Wilfredo informed her what her sister had told us and said we were there to help. She closed her eyes and shook her head, her black, curly hair bobbed as she said she couldn't talk to us, wouldn't talk to us, because her husband would kill her if she did.

Wilfredo dragged the chair across the room and placed it in front of her. I walked over and sat on the bed next to her, taking her hand in mine. Wilfredo pleaded with her to talk to us; he told her we were there to help. But she continued to shake her head and told us she had gone to the police many times and they did nothing to help her. Then he would beat her again and cut her legs with knives to punish her betrayal.

She stretched one of her legs forward and pulled up her pantleg, displaying cut after cut and said she could barely walk because of the wounds that patterned her legs.

"I've gone to the police many times," she said, "This is how they helped me, by doing nothing. This is what he does when I disobey him. He delights in cutting me. Now he wants to kill me, and I know he will do it. He has killed before."

I grabbed her other hand, and pulled her closer, twisting her body so she was facing me as we sat on the edge of the bed together.

"Those times," I said to her with force as tears welled in my eyes, "you went to the police. This time, God sent the police to you! We are here because God sent us here to help you."

Tears began to pour down her face, she bowed her shaking head to hide them and told us to go away. I wrapped my arms around her, ignoring the rancid smell of her sweaty body. I pushed back thoughts of bugs and whatever other creatures that might be living on her that might also be passing to my body and rocked her in my arms, speaking softly with words of assurance.

Wilfredo had been sitting on the chair watching us. He stood up, returned the chair to the corner. He said he was going to leave us alone to talk as he led the daughter toward the door. I heard the door close.

"Gloria, you don't have to live in fear. You don't have to stay in this shack terrified for your life. God loves you. He sent us to rescue you and to help you." I pleaded with her.

"You have a choice! You can stay here in the dark for the rest of your life, living in fear, or you can take my hand and receive God's rescue. You can step outside that door and leave the darkness behind forever. Step out into the sunshine, look up at that beautiful, clear-blue sky and grab your freedom."

She repeated that she couldn't leave this sanctuary because she would die. I told her to have faith, that God would protect her, we would protect her. But she didn't believe me.

I don't know how long we talked. In moments like this, it feels as though time is suspended. Was it an hour? A half hour? Longer? I don't know. But I prayed with her and talked with her, my voice soft and reassuring, like the trickle of a stream on a hot summer night, all the while rocking her body in my arms. The tears came like a storm during rainy season and her body convulsed in rhythm with her sobs.

I heard the door squeak open, saw the stream of light slither across the floor, but I ignored Wilfredo as he entered the room and walked over to stand silently in the corner. I heard the hushed voices of the others outside. Gloria reached for a dirty, torn piece of cloth on the bed. She lifted her face and wiped the tears; her wide eyes pierced me.

"I will tell you what happened, if you promise to protect me and my daughter."

During the next hour or so she gave a declaration to Wilfredo about the three murders her husband had committed: the man he knifed in Talanga, the man he killed in Tegucigalpa, the other lover he had who cheated on him. She told about the many times he cut her body with his knife to punish her for disobedience. She recounted the nights he viciously raped her to satisfy his needs.

She rose from the bed, turned her back to us, and lowered her blouse off her shoulders, revealing her back. She said her husband took his machete and carved his name in her back—twice—to mark her as his property and assure she was faithful to him because no other man would dare touch his possessions. Wilfredo and I sat in silent shock as we saw the scars on her back that spelled out her husband's name—twice.

While Gloria spoke with Wilfredo, her daughter sat on a bench in the sunshine outside giving her statement to another investigator about how her father had come to her bed at night and forced her to have sex with him. She talked about his abuse and violence in detail. Listening to them recount their tales of terror was like watching a flood of pain rolling through mountains, cleaning up the debris of their lives along its shore, sweeping it away, and leaving a fresh canvas of hope.

At this time in Honduras' history, there were no shelters, no refuges to which you could take a woman in danger to be safe. Ours didn't open until a year later.

About a twenty-minute drive through the mountains from where this shack stood, a friend of ours had a ministry. I called and asked him if they could hide Gloria and her daughter until we could finish the investigation, obtain the arrest warrant, and put the husband behind bars.

He told me no, that they were not prepared or outfitted for that kind of work. I begged and pleaded with him until he finally agreed to receive them into his care and protection.

When Gloria and her daughter were done with their declarations, it was time to leave. I knew Gloria was still afraid of walking out of that shack and the security it had afforded her during the prior month.

It has been more than a decade since that day, and I can still recall it clearly in my mind. I sat next to her on the bed while her daughter packed their clothes into sacks.

"You can do this," I told her, watching her eye the door as she gripped my hands tighter. "Breathe."

We stood and together, we slowly walked to the door that stood wide open, while police stood guard outside. I helped her as she hobbled on her crutches, taking tiny steps.

"You can do this," I repeated. "Freedom is waiting for you."

When we reached the door and the sunshine hit her face, she looked up to the heavens, took a deep breath, and looked at me with hesitation. I put my hand on her shoulder and told her it was safe. She stepped out into the sunshine and smiled.

Of all the work we have done, serving so many people, this was by far one of the most profound moments of my life. There was a connection of trust and faith between us that I have tried but failed to put words to because it is something so deep, there are no words.

Three months passed before the authorities were able to obtain the arrest warrant, find her husband and arrest him. During those three months, God worked a miracle in Gloria's life.

Our friend, who had been caring for her at his ministry, called a month after we dropped her off, saying we needed to come get her. She was sick, and they were not capable of caring for someone as ill as she was. She had a minor stroke and was partially paralyzed on one side of her body. She could not walk.

I told them I didn't know where we could put her and keep her safe, but I would try to find someone else to take her. A week passed and, to be honest, I ignored their calls because I could not find any other ministry who would take her. Then I received an urgent message to call them.

"She's been healed," said the excited voice on the other end of the telephone.

A stunned silence does not describe my reaction. It was more like the breath had been sucked out of my body and I could not speak. My mind, in this brief moment, could not grasp the reality of the words I had just heard.

Healed?

"We didn't know what to do," said the voice of my friend's assistant. "We were going to a revival at the stadium in Tegucigalpa and decided to take Gloria and her daughter with us. Something happened. She received Christ and wanted us to take her down to the altar for prayer. It was quite difficult because she hadn't been able to walk at all since her stroke."

I listened as a sense of overwhelming awe crept up on me.

"Some of the guys picked her up and carried her down," the voice continued. "The pastors prayed with her, laid hands on her, prayed over her for healing, and she *walked* back to her seat!"

"You mean they helped her walk back," I corrected.

"No . . . she walked back on her own. She doesn't even need her crutches anymore!"

There it was. Healing. I had to see this for myself. My son Dominic and I drove to where we were hiding her. We saw the miraculous power of a God who heals.

Her daughter ran to the gate to meet us when we arrived at the ministry two hours later. I confess I was doubting there had been a complete healing. In a distance I saw Gloria sitting on a chair on the porch of the rehab center while other clients walked around or sat in the shade on the lawn. I left my son and her daughter to chat with each other—they had become friends through this case—and I went to sit with Gloria and find out what happened.

Gloria rose as I approached, and she walked toward me. Her face shone brighter than the sun in the sky. Her steps were normal and smooth, not hesitant nor weak as they had been before. I looked for her crutches by her chair, but there weren't any. When she reached me, she grabbed me and hugged me with such force I could barely breathe. We embraced and rocked back and forth as both of us began to cry, this time, with tears of joy.

She was so happy. She told me about her struggle when she first arrived, about the stroke and her desire to leave because it had felt like no one wanted them there. She and her daughter had been attending Bible classes and rehab classes with the other clients and heard about the revival in Tegucigalpa. She said it had been a battle because of her medical condition to get them to approve her going to the event.

"I felt the love of God pour over me," she said. "I had to go down front and give my life. I knew God had rescued me. I wanted him to heal me too."

And he did. She no longer suffered pain. She could walk normally without her crutches. All the medical issues she had suffered were gone, and in the place of the old Gloria was a new Gloria giving meaning to her name, giving glory to God for all he had done for her.

The last time I saw Gloria was the day we recovered her from where we hid her and her daughter for three months until her husband's arrest and trial. We drove her to the courthouse in Talanga where she walked in unaided by those handmade crutches.

I don't know where those crutches went.

We sat with her and her daughter as they waited to testify. After court, we drove them to her family's house, where they had packed her personal things to transport her to another part of the country to start a new life.

I remember her smiling and laughing with us in the back seat of our truck while Officer Chavarria drove.

"Freedom smells so good," she said. She added that even though the *cicatrices* (scars) on her body would remain, she was healed and free from everything else.

As we parted ways, she thanked us for the help and told me to tell her story to others, so they would know there is "*una salida de la oscuridad*" (a way out of the darkness).

That afternoon as I walked to my office, I looked over to the jailcell where her husband was detained, awaiting transfer to Tamara, a Honduran prison in the same town where we found her hiding, where he was to serve a three-year sentence. I heard his voice, "*Gringa, voy a matarte por ese.*" It was a death threat. The first of many I have received.

I continued walking to my office as though I hadn't heard his words and shut the door. Like Gloria, I choose freedom. I choose to continue walking this path regardless of the dangers. Why? Because of women like Gloria. They have no one to help lift them out of the darkness.

Years later there would be a song called "No Longer Slaves" written by Jonathan and Melissa Helser, born out of their testimony and story. I remember Gloria whenever I hear that song and sing, "I'm no longer a slave to fear, I am a child of God . . . Love has called my name."

Love itself called Gloria's name.

SECTION III

OUR STRUGGLE IS NOT AGAINST FLESH AND BLOOD

CHAPTER NINE

PERSECUTION RISING

*"We are hard pressed on every side, but not crushed; perplexed
but not in despair; persecuted, but not abandoned;
struck down, but not destroyed . . ."*
2 Corinthians 4:8–9 (NIV)

You will never know if you have true courage until you find yourself
in the fire and realize you have no courage at all. It is in this moment
when, through faith, you take hold of the only source of true courage—a
Father who is all powerful and who cares for you in your trials and troubles.

It was normal, everyday living to receive death threats. Every time I left
the house, I prayed for safety. Lee stayed behind at the ministry or was in the
United States and prayed I would come home alive.

I detailed the first threat I can remember in the previous chapter when
Gloria's husband rasped from his jailcell as he awaited transfer to prison,
"Gringa, voy a matarte por ese."

But the first time—to my knowledge—that someone tried to murder
me was a different story. We had been in Guaimaca, a town forty kilometers
north of Talanga, in the high school teaching students about violence, rescue,
and prevention over the course of several days. We stayed in a hotel on the
park, so we wouldn't have to commute each day.

One morning as I crossed the park in search of coffee, a teacher, who was also a local television host, stopped me.

"Gracie, we need your help," Orlando said, looking nervously around. "A mother called me who has a son, about twelve, who can barely walk. An American missionary took him to Tegucigalpa and sexually abused him."

I listened to the story of how the missionary, Daniel, told the boy's mother he would take her son to the capital city for a bike, clothes, and pizza. For more than three days, the mother worried about her son because they had not returned. Each time she asked the pastor of the church where Daniel worked about her son and Daniel, she was told not to worry, and that they would be home soon.

Orlando told me that the police in Tegucigalpa had called the pastor when they found the boy wandering the streets late at night. The pastor went to Tegucigalpa and brought him home. A day or so later, the mother told the pastor her son didn't seem right, he was bleeding from his rear end and could barely walk or sit. The pastor told her to be quiet and not say anything because they would receive no more help from the church if she said anything to anyone.

But the boy's mother could not keep quiet. She contacted Orlando, who daily receives public *denuncias* (reports) on his television show. He was known in the community as a person who sought truth and justice and tried to help the people.

I called my office in Talanga and told them a case was coming in, then told Orlando to take the mother and the boy directly to my office. What ensued was a hunt to find Daniel, who had fled Tegucigalpa when the boy escaped the hotel room in which he had been held hostage and abused. Authorities finally encountered Daniel in the northern part of the country and transported him to Talanga.

A media storm ensued.

An American missionary sexually abusing a boy was big news. The media wanted a comment each time I stepped onto the street. One time, the same journalist who had asked me why I hated men, approached me, put his live camera in my face, and asked, "What do you think about your countryman being accused of raping a child? Will you be helping him?"

He was always looking for a way to sabotage the work, and me personally. But in the culture in which I was living, the question had merit. With levels of corruption so high, it was known that friends and family helped each other out, even if one was accused of raping a boy. What he didn't know was that I wasn't like that. I didn't know this man, even though he was a missionary and was an American. If I did, I would not have acted any different.

"Let me say this," I replied, "I am ashamed that a man from my country would come here in the name of God and do such a horrible thing. I guarantee you that not only will I work this case as hard as I do the others, but even harder because what he did disgusts me as an American and as a Christian."

I walked away.

We had him, and court day arrived. In Honduras the preliminary court proceeding must occur within the first seven days after an arrest. Also, criminal court must be held in the same jurisdiction in which the crime occurred. Daniel was in a Talanga jailcell, but the crime occurred in a hotel in Tegucigalpa, meaning court was going to be held in the capital city.

The prosecutor from Tegucigalpa arrived early that morning with two officers for security. However, the boy, his mother, and the witnesses could not all fit in their passenger car. We did not have our truck yet, but I spoke with a cab driver we knew well who offered to transport the witnesses in his cab. The prosecutor gave us one of her officers for security and we prepared to leave. Daniel would ride handcuffed in the truck bed of the *patrulla* about twenty minutes behind us.

We didn't know people were watching us and planning to take us out before we ever made it to the court. The road to Tegucigalpa from Talanga was a fifty-four-kilometer, two-lane road through the mountains, mostly unpopulated.

There were many steep drops and hairpin curves on the winding road, with barely enough space for vehicles to pass each other. Drivers would hug the edge of the road and pray they didn't hit gravel or sideswipe oncoming vehicles. There was no emergency lane on the side of the road, which was filled with potholes and sunken dips.

We left Talanga with the prosecutor's car leading us and sped through the mountain roads on the way to the city. The first vehicle contained the prosecutor, her officer, who was driving, and the boy and his mother. In our vehicle I sat in the passenger seat next to the taxi driver and the officer sat in the back with the two witnesses.

We were about halfway to the city when I first saw them: A pickup on the side of the road under a tree that appeared to be suspended onto the side of the cliff that dropped several hundred feet to the valley below. The truck bed was loaded with men and others inside. Alarms began ringing in my spirit as we approached, and I immediately looked at the license plate and began reciting its number in my head.

As we approached, I observed the driver sitting sideways looking over his left shoulder down the road at us. His right hand was on the ignition, and when we passed, his eyes locked with mine and I saw him turn the keys in the ignition. I began shouting at the officer to keep an eye on them and searched for a pen and paper on which to write the plate number.

We cruised past the summit and began the winding descent on the other side when suddenly two pickups filled with men began to pass us. I don't know where the second one came from. Most likely it had been following us from Talanga.

The first tried to push between us and the prosecutor's car to separate us, and the second edged closer to the left side of our vehicle, trying to push us off the road into the drop-offs on the right.

Time shifted into slow motion as though we were in an action film. All I remember from that moment was yelling at the driver to keep our nose in the backside of the car in front of us and to not let our wheels hit the gravel on the right side of our car. I began praying but kept my eyes on the truck trying to push us off the road. The officer in the back threw his body over the witnesses to protect them. Up and around and down we went. I heard the gravel crunching under our right tires.

We began to climb a hill, and I looked up and saw the most welcome sight I had ever seen. An enormous and overloaded dump truck topped the hill and was racing down toward us at high speed. I praised God and turned to look at the pickups. The men saw the dump truck too.

I held my breath, closed my eyes, braced, and prayed because we had only seconds until impact. I waited for the bang and jolt that was inevitable.

Nothing happened.

I opened my eyes as we topped the hill. The drivers in the pickups had hit their brakes hard and fallen way behind us to avoid a head-on with the dump truck or losing control and running off the road. We sped through the remaining mountains at more than a hundred and forty kilometers an hour and never saw those guys again. Daniel was convicted, sent to prison, and we went home later that afternoon.

God sent a dump truck to save us. I truly believe that. If it had not topped that hill at that exact moment, we would have been pushed off the side of that mountain. Today the road is wider and better. But each time I pass that spot, I remember God's faithfulness and rescue . . . and his dump truck.

A friend who read this story for feedback asked a good question: "Why would these guys want to kill you for bringing an American rapist missionary to be punished?"

Each case is a battle in Honduras. Families and friends of the accused fervently believe he or she is innocent. Some cases are quiet and relatively uneventful. Others are battles for justice and a struggle to survive until justice is served. It doesn't matter if there are video recordings, witnesses, or DNA evidence. It is, in their minds, our fault—or mine to be exact—that their friend, son, or brother is going to prison.

In some cases there are bribes, in some, threats, and sometimes people are on the move to take out the victim, the witnesses, and me. They believe by doing so, the accused will go free.

It was a few months later that the second attempt on my life happened. A young woman from the village of La Branza, a tiny community west of Talanga, came into our office with her father. She was badly beaten by her husband, who was a taxi driver in Tegucigalpa. He was also involved with one of the deadliest gangs in Central America.

She had left him and gone to her family's home in the mountains north of the capital. Again, because the abuse happened in the capital city where she had lived with him, we had to bring her case to the court there.

The special domestic violence judge in the Supreme Court building in Tegucigalpa upheld her case and put in a protection order as well as a visitation schedule for their child. The husband continued to abuse and threaten her and her family by phone and during visits with his three-year-old son. He even showed up at her parents' house, violating the protection order.

We called the judge in Tegucigalpa, and she told us to have the woman and her father come to the court the next morning to file charges, raising the case to criminal status. The next morning she, her son, and her father took the bus to the capital city.

It was afternoon when her father walked into my office—alone and bleeding. He told me that as they exited the bus in the city, her husband and gang members beat him severely and kidnapped his daughter and grandson.

We had to move fast with the authorities. By law the husband could be arrested for the kidnapping and the assault if we found and caught him within twenty-four hours of the event. We assembled a team of two officers from the intelligence department and Officers Sanchez and Chavarria, who worked with us and took the father back to the capital to file a report in the prosecutor's office in the sector where the assault and kidnapping occurred. Then we put the father back on a bus to Talanga and began hunting for the husband.

It was about two in the morning in a very dangerous section of the capital city that we found him with his wife and son. He was arrested and transported to the Metro 1 jail and we took the woman and her son to her sister's house on the edge of the capital to hide out until they saw the judge the next day. We returned to Talanga just before dawn to rest before we returned to Tegucigalpa for court the next afternoon.

While I was in the judge's chambers with our client the next afternoon, my officers were waiting outside—with my phone. The judge and I struggled to persuade the woman to go somewhere else with her son, but she was adamantly against the idea.

"My family called from Talanga this morning," she said. "A gang member grabbed my younger brother outside his school and threatened to kill me and my family if I didn't return to my husband with my son."

We offered to help find a place for her and her son to hide, but she was overwhelmed with concern for her family. After more than an hour, we had to resign ourselves to the fact she would not accept our assistance, not because she didn't want it, but because she was afraid someone in her family would be hurt, or die, if she did.

My officers were in a panic when we came out of the judge's chambers. They said my phone had been ringing like crazy and that her sister had called saying the husband was at her house banging on the door screaming that he and all the gang members were "looking for that damn *gringa* and her police officers." He promised torture and death when they found us.

We hadn't known he had been released. Law required him to be held for twenty-four hours, but he had been released within six hours of his detention. We don't know why, but we assume either someone was stupid, they knew someone and pulled some strings, or they were paid or threatened to let him out.

I can still see her standing on the top steps of the Supreme Court building in Tegucigalpa as we pulled away: pathetic, broken, lost, and without hope. That was the last time I saw her.

To the right of where she stood was a statue of Blind Lady Justice with her scales. Isaiah 59:9–11 (NIV) came to mind: "So justice is far from us, and righteousness does not reach us. We look for light, but all is darkness; for brightness, but we walk in deep shadows. Like the blind we grope along the wall, feeling our way like men without eyes. At midday we stumble as if it were twilight; among the strong we are like the dead . . . We look for justice, but find none; for deliverance, but it is far away."

We left her there because we had other things to deal with and needed to quickly leave.

My officers shoved a bulletproof vest over my head and tossed me in the backseat of our truck and told me to stay on the floor. We didn't know if the husband or gang members were around the court building waiting for us to leave. Because they had let her husband out so early, he didn't know, or at least we hoped he didn't know, that we had a court date with the judge.

Calls continued to come in to my phone that we were being hunted and our truck was well known. My officers raced through afternoon traffic while I covered us in prayer. We headed straight for Casamata, national police headquarters, where they let us in the back gate and took us to one of the generals' offices.

Myrna, I love her. She was one of the few women in Honduras to become a general and she fervently supported our work since it began. She sarcastically asked me what kind of trouble I had gotten us into this time and grew serious as the officers explained the situation. She called the colonel in Talanga to coordinate our safe journey home.

I looked at my officers and we all held our breath. We had a new colonel whom I had only met briefly when he was transferred to Talanga a few days before. He hadn't been briefed on this case, but his second-in-command knew everything, including that we were given the team to hunt this guy down the night before.

What a way to be introduced to your new colonel . . . his superior calls him to tell him we are in trouble and orders him to collaborate and do whatever necessary to keep us safe. I was cringing, thinking of the disapproval that might be waiting for me when I returned to the office and faced him.

The plan to safely get us through the mountains and back to Talanga was to send us with a heavily armed escort by back mountain roads through the Valley of Angels instead of the direct route. A *patrulla* full of police and Cobras (national swat/special forces) would escort us to the Valley of Angels. There, in coordination with our new colonel, a *patrulla* also filled with police and Cobras would deliver us safely to Talanga.

Chavarria, one of my officers, was off duty at 6 p.m. and was due for his annual physical evaluation at headquarters early the next morning, so he stayed in the city. That meant I had to do the driving home while Officer Sanchez kept vigilance on the way. Our trip to the Valley of Angels was uneventful, and we arrived at the station safely after dark as it began to rain.

Calls were made to the colonel in Talanga, and we were handed off from one group to another to continue our journey. Rain began to furiously fall as we left the station.

The Valley of Angels (*Valle de Ángeles*) is a mountain community about a mile above sea level known as the valley where the angels live. An old Spanish Colonial town, it is now an arts community and place where visitors go to eat and buy things such as wood carvings, artwork, jewelry, and textiles. The roads we would travel from there to Cantarranas were steep, narrow, and with some of the tightest hairpin curves I have driven in Honduras. I love driving this road for its challenge.

As we reached the last peak in the mountains before a long descent into the valley, a truck full of men pulled between us and the *patrulla* behind. Each time the *patrulla* full of officers and Cobras tried to pass it, the vehicle blocked them. Officer Sanchez told me to hit the gas.

I can honestly say I have never come down that mountain as fast as I did that night. My pistol, which was under my right thigh, almost slid out onto the floor several times as I pushed the clutch and the brake, shifting gears. On a good day, one could travel at forty kilometers an hour (25 mph) up or down the mountain. But we were traveling in the dark, in the pouring rain between eighty and ninety kilometers per hour (50-55 mph). The *patrulla* and the truck disappeared behind us. We called ahead to the Cantarranas police; they had a *patrulla* filled with officers waiting at the bottom of the mountain.

A few minutes after reaching the bottom, the *patrulla* that had been following us arrived, the officers saying they had to put sirens and lights on the truck to get the other vehicle full of men out of their way. They weren't sure if it was a problem or not, but they were not going to take chances. They decided with their bigger force to wait at the bottom of the mountain and send us with the Cantarranas officers to Talanga.

The new colonel wasn't happy when we arrived around nine that night. During debrief he did have an officer bring me some fried chicken and coffee, but he restricted me to the station for the night. I had to sleep on a foam cushion on the floor of my office, so he could, as he stated, "Obey the general and keep [me] safe since [I] got [myself] into such trouble."

He did allow me to go home the next evening but assigned Officer Sanchez to stay with me at the mission house in La Ermita. This was before we built the center. At that time the only building on the property was my house with a chain-link fence. After three days I sent Officer Sanchez back to headquarters as he was getting on my nerves. I just wanted to be alone and have some quiet.

Again, the Lord protected us . . . and it would not be the last time.

CHAPTER TEN

THE BEGINNING OF THE END
(OF THE BEGINNING)

"Therefore we do not lose heart . . . For our light and
momentary troubles are achieving for us an eternal glory that
far outweighs them all. So we fix our eyes not on what is seen,
but on what is unseen . . ."
2 Corinthians 4:16–18 (NIV)

Sometimes it appears all is lost, when God is doing exactly what needs to be done. It appears the battle is lost, when victory is a bit further down the path on the journey.

Police officers in Honduras are frequently moved around, rotating from one assignment to another. In the United States and many other countries, police live in their communities and go home after their shifts. But officers in Honduras are assigned posts that often are hours from home. They live at their posts and only go home for two days every fifteen days. Some live so far from their posts they can only be with their families during vacations or Easter, Christmas, and New Year's holidays when they are given three or four days off.

This presented difficulties for our project because we constantly needed to orient new colonels and officers about our work. It is the same with judges and prosecutors. In one way it was good, because when they moved to other areas of the country, they helped expand the model.

But during early 2010 the rotations became downright dangerous. It was March when they placed a colonel in Talanga who was different from the others with whom we previously had worked.

On the day he was installed in Talanga, I was briefly introduced to him before the transfer-of-power ceremony. Afterwards, Colonel Quintin, the outgoing colonel, brought me into his office to formally present me to the new colonel. It was shortly before Holy Week, when half of the officers would be on leave for four days before returning to duty to allow the other half of the police to take their four-day holiday leaves.

The three of us sat in the office, the new colonel at the desk and Colonel Quintin and I on the couches. Colonel Quintin explained our work and the support we had from national police headquarters and the minister of security. When it was my turn to speak, I explained how we worked with cases involving special victims, assisting victims during and after their crises, supervising their cases, and providing logistic support to the authorities.

Leaning back in his chair, the new colonel (for personal safety and security issues we will call him Colonel O) asked for more specifics on the cases we were involved in. I began detailing the various cases, such as domestic and family violence, child sexual abuse, prostitution of minors, and sex trafficking. Nodding his head in agreement, he appeared friendly and supportive. But when I added that we also worked with families and authorities in cases of murder and kidnapping involving vulnerable groups, his attitude changed.

"Why do you have anything to do with kidnapping?" Colonel O asked, his voice raised.

I was taken aback, but remained silent as did Colonel Quinton, who I believe also was shocked by the reaction.

Colonel O's thin face reddened with rage and his hands tightly gripped the arms of his chair.

Colonel Quintin began to explain how our work covered all cases of violence against members of vulnerable social groups. I added that our role in such kidnapping cases was to provide logistical support to the *Anti-Secuestro* (anti-kidnapping) unit in Tegucigalpa.

Colonel O again leaned back in his chair, intently listening with his hands folded together, thumbs under his chin.

"Last year," I said, "we had a case in which an eighteen-month-old baby, who was also a United States citizen, had been kidnapped. His father was Honduran and lived in Oregon. His mother was also Honduran. She had been in the United States without a visa when she gave birth but had come back to Honduras when her mother became ill. Then her baby had been kidnapped for ransom. We worked with the special unit providing housing, transportation, and food while they worked the case and we provided emotional, logistical, and spiritual support to the mother.

"As a result of our collaboration," I continued, "we were able to rescue the baby, even after an uncle had been murdered by the kidnappers."

Colonel O was silent, seething with anger. His cellphone rang, and after he took the call he dismissed me, saying we would talk more later. I left his office and went downstairs to mine to work with Karina, a woman we employed as our victims' advocate. Later that afternoon I saw Colonel O enter his personal vehicle and leave the compound. Colonel Quintin left after the meeting to go to his new assignment.

During the next few days I asked the sergeant in reception if the colonel was in, so we could review some of our cases but was told he wasn't in. After three days I asked when he would be back, and the sergeant told me he would return the next week.

That Friday evening I was home early and was relaxing when a woman I knew from the village came to the door with her daughter. Both appeared terrified, their hair and clothes disheveled, and their faces covered in smudges from tears mixed with dirt. I could see the beginning of bruises blooming on her arms.

The woman said her husband had beaten her and was looking for her to kill her. I told her she needed to report it to the police in the post across the street. They would help and protect her. I was tired and honestly didn't want to leave the house to accompany her to the post, so I sent her off and said if she needed anything else, she should let me know.

A while later my cellphone rang. It was the sergeant from the post. He said he wasn't sure about the procedures in a domestic violence case and asked me to come help him. I looked at my hot supper on the coffee table, remembering this was the first time in a couple weeks I was home to eat supper, knowing that if I went to the post I could be gone for hours.

"I will be right over," I said as I grabbed my sweater, the domestic violence law booklet, and my keys.

As I walked into the police post, an adobe building—except for the portion we built with blocks back in 2005—with a ceramic tile roof and cement floor, I heard the woman crying and her husband shouting. I was surprised he was in the post. The walls in the reception room had been painted years ago, its color faded, the brittle, off-white paint peeling. In the middle of the room were a dented grey, metal desk, a tall filing cabinet with an old television on top of it, and three white, plastic chairs. To the right, against the wall, was an old, wooden bench.

The sergeant jumped up from behind the desk and used an old towel to wipe clean the one empty plastic chair next to the crying woman. I looked at the husband, who was handcuffed, sitting on the bench against the wall. He erupted with a litany of loud claims about his wife's alleged transgressions, insisting his wife was blowing the incident out of proportion, peppering his monologue with machoistic insults aimed at shutting up his wife.

"*Clase*," I calmly said to the sergeant, using the formal way of addressing one of his rank. "You can't have this husband sitting here continuing to victimize her. The law states that if he is arrested within twenty-four hours of the violent act, he needs to be held for twenty-four hours in the jailcell. This happened half an hour ago, and he is continuing to berate her in front of us."

I opened my little book on the domestic violence law and showed the regulation to the sergeant. The man quieted and glared at me. The sergeant realized I was right and took the man out back, put him in the jailcell, and returned to his desk. During the next hour I helped him fill out the domestic violence report form and the *medidas de seguridad* (protection order).

I also explained he needed to bring the man and the report to the judge in Talanga in the morning because reports must be submitted within twenty-four hours of reception. Because the man was in custody, the judge could hold the hearing in the morning. I turned to the woman and told her to go to the judge in the morning. I showed them both the procedures clearly written out in the law book.

About noon the next day the sergeant called me agitated and upset. He said Colonel O had ripped up the *medidas de seguridad* and the domestic violence report, released the husband from custody, then publicly berated the woman in front of the police station.

In addition, Colonel O was punishing the sergeant because, as he quoted the colonel, "Only the DNIC (investigators) can take a domestic violence report and no *gringa* can tell police what to do or to arrest someone."

He added that the colonel wanted to speak with me.

Although I was confident the procedures had been properly executed, and optimistic I could straighten the situation out, the moment turned out to be a foreshadowing to how the following year would progress.

When I arrived at police headquarters, I approached the wife, who was sitting on the bench in the patio area in front of reception. Sobbing, she told me how her husband was furious with her and that she was overwhelmed with shame for the scandal unfolding in public that morning. I told her I would go talk with the colonel and rectify the matter.

Colonel O was seething when I entered his office. He was a small man, short and thin, but muscular, his close-cut hair more gray than dark. I greeted him and sat on the couch in front of his desk. What followed was like something out of an overly dramatic war movie in which a martinet of a commanding officer verbally berates a hapless subordinate.

"You have no authority to order an arrest," he shouted through gritted teeth, the veins in his neck pulsing. "The police cannot take a domestic violence report, only the DNIC can do that!" He tossed his hands in the air. "Why is there a *gringa* even in this police headquarters?"

"The law changed in 2007," I said, trying to calm him. "Police can take a domestic violence report, even I can. It must be submitted to the judge within twenty-four hours. The police and DNIC can immediately issue a temporary protection order for two months and part of that protection order includes arresting the aggressor and detaining him for twenty-four hours as a calming-down period."

He was silent, but I could sense the rage building within him.

"I have been extensively trained by your government," I added, "to teach the police and other authorities."

In response he leaned forward in his chair, eyes blazing.

"Are you telling me that you know more about the law than I do?"

I realized I needed a reply to calm the situation, not anger him any further. Alarm bells were ringing in my spirit.

"You have so many things to know," I started. "I only focus on a few of the laws, and because I do, I know them well. The laws are always changing, and it could be easy to miss one. I have copies of the new domestic violence law in my office and would be glad to give you one. But yes, police can take the report and put in the protection order."

My response did not calm him. If he hadn't been gripping the arms of his chair as tightly as he was, I believe he would have come over the top of his desk and physically assaulted me.

"You will not be telling any police officer what to do," he shouted. "You do not belong here! Get out of my office and don't cause me any more problems."

I skittered out of there as fast as I could without appearing to be escaping from him and went directly below to the office in which I worked.

"Please take a copy of the new domestic violence law up to the colonel," I told Karina. "I am going home."

On my way out, an officer pulled me aside and warned me that I needed to be very careful with this colonel. He didn't like what we were doing and didn't like me being there. He also told me that during morning assembly he had been asking the officers in formation about the officers assigned in our office, their identities and whereabouts. No one volunteered information. It was Holy Week and my two guys were on their days off. They'd be returning in a couple of days.

A couple of days later, another officer came into our office about a domestic violence case. A man had badly beaten his wife a few days before and the DNIC had taken her report but didn't put in a protection order. The man continued to call, show up, and insult his wife. That morning he had gone to her house and taken away her infant. The officer wanted to know what to do.

I explained to him—and showed him the law—that part of the protection order, which the DNIC was obligated to issue but failed to do, was to recuperate the minors and put them in the mother's custody until the case went to court. Being Holy Week, the court was closed, and the cases could not be submitted to the court until the Monday after Easter even though the law required it to be remitted within twenty-four hours.

"We should go get the baby," the officer said.

Remembering the fiasco in the colonel's office, I suggested he take a copy of the law up to the colonel and ask permission to use a *patrulla* to go get the baby and put in the protection order, which the man was violating. The officer informed me the colonel had left the night before and would not be back until later in the week. He suggested we ask the second-in-command, who always collaborated with us.

The second-in-command agreed we needed to get the baby for the woman, but no *patrullas* were available. He sent the officer, the woman, and me with another female officer in our ministry truck to put in force the protection order and recover the child.

I drove. When we arrived at the pig farm a few minutes outside Talanga where the man was staying, the mother and I remained in the truck while the officers went to do their job. Normally I don't leave the truck until they have everything under control. It's a security issue. They recovered the child, although the man's family members weren't happy about it, the protection order was issued, and we left.

When we returned to police headquarters, I saw Sanchez, one of the officers assigned to our office, and he pulled me aside to talk in private. He told me he had learned that the colonel, who was still away from headquarters, had been asking about the officers assigned to the *gringa's* office.

"Trouble is brewing," Officer Sanchez said, leaning close so others would not hear him speak. "Be careful."

The next few days passed quietly and uneventful. Colonel O returned on Sunday (Easter) night. On Monday morning his second-in-command warned me the colonel was on the warpath. He already had reassigned the officers who had been assigned to our office, transferring one to another post an hour away and the other to patrol duty. Also, the colonel had learned I had helped officers recover a baby. He reprimanded the two officers and his second-in-command.

It was the first time in almost five years that police were not assigned to the office. The only people in the victim's office were two civilians: our advocate, Karina, and me. Thus began eighteen months of battle, sabotage attempts, attacks, and a constant struggle to keep the work going.

Of course, it wasn't only this colonel who didn't like our work. There were others. In addition to aggressors and their friends and family, there were also various investigators, a couple of prosecutors, and a judge.

It is difficult to cope with the idea of people hating you, especially when everything you do and sacrifice is to help others. I wanted people to like and respect me. The rejection was painful. I believed if Colonel O took the opportunity to get to know us better, learn more about our work and how our successes made him look better to his superiors, things would improve.

After patiently and silently bearing with him screaming at me for working with the police to recover the baby, I asked him if he could find time to sit down and allow me to explain our purpose more in depth and share the testimony of God's work. He said he would let me know.

A few days later, Karina called saying Colonel O wanted to meet us at a restaurant outside Talanga at seven that evening. He said we could explain everything then. I didn't like the idea of meeting at night, away from the office and the police station, but I believed he was giving us an opportunity and didn't want to miss it.

Karina lived two houses south of our ministry in La Ermita. I picked her up just before seven, and we drove to the restaurant. It was closed. We looked at each other, wondering what to do and called the colonel. He told us to pick another restaurant and call him back when we knew where we would meet.

Nothing, or almost nothing is open after dark in Honduras. In the few large cities, malls and restaurants stay open during evening hours. By seven or eight, towns and villages are eerie ghost towns. It is too dangerous to be out and about. No buses or taxis are in service and few people owned vehicles then. These days more people have motorcycles, but back in 2010, no one could travel after dark unless it was by foot or bicycle.

Only one restaurant was open at seven on the main street in Talanga. We went inside and called the colonel. We called the new head of investigation for Talanga, a wonderful woman with the rank of Inspector. For her safety, we will call her *Inspectora*. She had arrived the week before and was amazing to work with. She joined us at the restaurant because she wanted to help explain our work to the colonel.

About a half hour later, a *patrulla* pulled up to the curb in front of the restaurant and Colonel O, in uniform, stepped out and came in. The odor of whiskey hit us before he reached the table and sat down. All three of us looked at each other as he shouted for the owner to come over and asked her what alcohol she had to serve. She said she only had beer.

"Nothing harder?" he growled in a loud, rude voice.

I could see he was drunk, in uniform, and had been driving the police truck. She brought him a beer and told him she was closing as it was getting near eight, so we needed to order our food fast. He announced we would not be eating anything.

The next forty-five minutes were a nightmare. Instead of talking about the program, Colonel O began to tell us how rich he was, where he lived in Tegucigalpa, and that we should come to his house to visit him. It was as though he was trying to seduce all three of us. He told us he had residency in the United States and frequently traveled to Miami.

Finally the owner came over, gave us our bill, and reminded us that she needed to close the restaurant. We left without dinner, having only had a soda each, except for the colonel who drank down two beers and left us to pay for them.

The next day I found out from other officers where Colonel O had been before he met up with us. He had dined in the home of a man we knew to be involved with drug, arms, and sex traffickers. His house—police officers who were forced to guard events there reported—was a frequent location for parties featuring drugs and prostitutes.

With Colonel O in charge, every day was like walking a tightrope. He ordered police not to pass victims to our office at headquarters; they were instructed to lie and say we were not there. Those who helped us were reprimanded.

The only bright spot at that time was the *Inspectora*, who had been at the restaurant with us. She helped us advocate for victims and make progress in their cases. But that didn't last for long because she was transferred to Tegucigalpa after a few months.

Many nights I prayed and prayed for God to help us. I couldn't see how to overcome this situation. The leaders in Tegucigalpa wanted to help us, but they couldn't control the colonel, and no one transferred him. There were days I felt as though I was sitting in the middle of a viper's nest. I could not understand why God wasn't moving this mountain.

A few months later, an American missionary friend, who lived in Tegucigalpa, called and we were talking about projects, prayer life, and other things. Before our call ended, Carol asked me to pray for her landlord's son. He had been kidnapped and she feared for his life. While his parents were Honduran, he was an American citizen. They had residency and he had been born and raised mostly in the United States.

A day or two later, Karina told me that the prior afternoon a vehicle matching the description of the car used in the kidnapping of the landlord's son passed in front of the police headquarters. One of the Inspectors spotted it and tried to get a *patrulla* and officers together to chase it down. However, everyone was reticent to comply with him because Colonel O had ordered them not to pursue the vehicle should it be seen in the area. By the time the inspector was able to get a group of willing officers together to pursue the car, they were unable to find it.

Shortly thereafter, as I read the morning paper in my office, I spotted an article about the same kidnapping. There was a picture of the abandoned vehicle, a white four-door on the side of the road, its doors open with a flat tire. The story said it had been abandoned in Agua Blanca, a village just outside Talanga. The article said that when the police found the vehicle and searched the surrounding area, nobody could be found.

Later that afternoon my cellphone rang. A female voice asked for me.

"My house is next door to the property where that white car was found," she said. "The police didn't search it enough. There is another building on the property where the kidnappers are with that young man."

I ran to reception and handed the cellphone to the sergeant, telling him what I had learned, and I asked him to return the phone to me once he gathered more information. He later brought it to me and said a group of officers had dispatched to see if the information was correct.

What he didn't tell me was that he had taken my cellphone to Colonel O for the informant to speak directly with him. Later in the afternoon, the *patrulla* came back without the victim or his captors. Officers said the other building was abandoned.

Two days later, the national news media reported the kidnapping victim had been murdered and his body dumped in Tegucigalpa in front of the public hospital's morgue. The family was devastated and so was my friend.

A feeling that something wasn't right gnawed at me.

A couple of weeks later, while I was in the investigative offices with a victim, I ran into a group of internal affairs officers from Tegucigalpa looking through files. They were investigating the kidnapping case. I told them about the vehicle supposedly passing in front of the police station and about the call I had received. They pulled me into a room to speak privately and said the colonel was under investigation in relation to this case.

Nothing ever happened with that investigation. Nothing ever happens with any investigation against any high-ranking person in Honduras. Corruption is the operating system. If you have money and connections, you can get almost anything you want. If you stood up against the system or got in anyone's way—they made sure you got out of the way.

Another kidnapping came to my attention a couple of months later. A man was kidnapped from Yoro, a town in a state by the same name that sits at the northern tip of Francisco Morazán and is famous for "*La Lluvia de Peces.*" It is a place where locals say fish fall from the sky during strong storms. A national bulletin was issued listing the description of the kidnappers and the vehicle used in the crime. Colonel Antonio, one of the good colonels we had worked with previously, was chief there and had mentioned it during one of our frequent telephone conversations.

About a week later, as I drove out of the ministry's driveway on my way to the police station, the sergeant from our village's post waved to me to stop and ran over, holding a folder under his arm. He was heading to Talanga for his daily report with the colonel and wanted to know if I could give him a ride, so he didn't have to take the bus.

Not every post has a vehicle. Most have no vehicle at all, one of the reasons helping victims was so difficult. The authorities did not have the resources they needed to do their jobs.

I really loved this sergeant. He was like an uncle to me, a fatherly figure who always smiled. But that day he wasn't smiling, and he looked tired. I asked him if he was sick, but he said no. As we traveled through the village, he asked me if I had heard about the kidnapping in Yoro. I told him that I had spoken with Colonel Antonio, who was chief in Yoro, and he had mentioned it.

"Did you see our *operativo* in the road the other day?" he asked.

I nodded, and he continued.

"We stopped a car that matched the description of the vehicle. In the back seat were three men. The one in the middle matched the description of the kidnapping victim."

"You're a hero!" I exclaimed. "You rescued him. I am so proud of you."

The sergeant became quiet and fiddled with the manila folder in his hands as we crossed the bridge exiting the village. He adjusted the buttons on his shirt and straightened his badge.

"I am sure it was him," he said. "But we didn't rescue him."

"I don't understand. What happened?"

"We were a bit confused too."

Then he explained that the driver was dressed in uniform—one of a high-ranking police officer. The sergeant had called Colonel O in Talanga and was told to let the vehicle go. He said he told the colonel that the vehicle and the victim matched the description of the alert, but he was ordered to let it pass and told not to take any information from them.

"Why didn't you call above him to Tegucigalpa?" I asked.

He turned to face me from the passenger seat.

"You never disobey the order of a superior officer or go above his head. You are severely punished if you do."

"Even if the superior is doing something that looks wrong, or that you believe to be criminal?"

"You never disobey a *jefe*," he said.

The word *jefe* is a term used to name a superior. We rode the rest of the way to Talanga in silence. Thinking back on it, I believe the sergeant purposely told me what happened. I believe he was warning me about Colonel O.

It was not the only time I was warned about this man and the danger he posed.

CHAPTER ELEVEN

ENEMIES WITHIN

*"He has delivered us from such a deadly peril, and he will
deliver us again. On him we have set our hope
that he will continue to deliver us."*
2 Corinthians 1:10 (NIV)

T hey say what you don't know can't hurt you. In certain situations,
however, knowing can save your life. We were surrounded by enemies.

One would think that when you serve others, they would realize you
are helping them. And perhaps they do . . . until your help hurts their
pocketbook. When your actions interrupt the capacity of corrupt people to
make illicit money, or threatens to expose their wrongdoings, you no longer
are an asset; you are a liability.

The international community considers Honduras to be one of the most
dangerous and corrupt places on Earth. At the time Colonel O was in charge
in Talanga, it was the murder capital of the world. It still is one of the world's
most dangerous places.

"World Report 2017,"[1] issued by Human Rights Watch, states in its
section "Countries—Honduras," pp. 309–310:

---

1   *Human Rights Watch World Report 2017* (Human Rights Watch, 2017).

"Rampant crime and impunity for human rights abuses remain the norm in Honduras . . . the murder rate is among the highest in the world . . . Efforts to reform the institutions responsible for providing public security have made little progress. Marred by corruption and abuse, the judiciary and police remain largely ineffective . . . Investigations into police abuses are hindered by inefficiency and corruption; little information about them is made public, and impunity is the rule . . . Judges face politically motivated intimidation and interference . . ."

The IACHR described Honduras in August [2016] as 'one of the most hostile and dangerous countries for human rights defenders.'"

"The Amnesty International Report 2016–2017, The State of the World's Human Rights,"[2] p. 24 says:

"The Americas remained one of the world's most violent regions . . . Central America's Northern Triangle of El Salvador, Guatemala, and Honduras was one of the world's most violent places, with more people killed there than in most conflict zones globally."

On August 19, 2018, *El Tiempo*, a Honduran newspaper, reported that Honduras was number one in rape cases in Latin America.

As I told you in the beginning, if we had known before we came, we probably never would have come.

But God works in us little by little, sometimes with baby steps. He nurtures us as he grows us into destiny. The years 2009 through 2011 were our most dangerous and difficult years. But having walked with God in this work, I had learned daily to lean on him, to trust in him, and to listen for his voice and guidance. I had begun to spiritually mature in a way I didn't realize until I looked back on it years later.

---

2   *Amnesty International Report 2017: The State of the World's Human Rights* (Amnesty International Ltd., 2017).

The trouble didn't begin with Colonel O's arrival in early 2010. It had always been there in the background but began to intensify regarding our relationships with the DNIC (investigative department of the police) and the *fiscalia* (prosecutor's office) as 2009 ended. The regular police never had been a problem for us. They loved the work. But there is a different dynamic in the investigative section of the police which, due to the nature of their work, opened the door to corruption.

Cases don't proceed when an investigation is stalled or thrown by the wayside. The police intervene when violence occurs, but the investigators are the ones who do the legwork and bring the case into the hands of the prosecutor. If the prosecutor never receives the case, all is lost. The dynamics of investigation provide fertile ground for seeds of corruption to sprout like weeds within a department.

Investigators have many moments alone with victims, witnesses, and perpetrators. Behind closed doors and through cellphone communication, there is great opportunity to offer payoffs and issue threats. When an investigator earns 15,000 lempiras a month ($625), it is tempting to accept bribes from drug traffickers, rapists, and other corrupt individuals. Interviews in back rooms of the station are prime opportunities to give and receive bribes.

Back in November 2009, during the political crisis, I had a showdown with the investigative office. It was called the DNIC at that time—*Dirección Nacional de Investigación Criminal.* Now it has a new name and acronym, DPI—*Departamento Policial de Investigación.*

We constantly butted heads with various DNIC investigators over mishandled special-victim cases. Many times when victims or their families showed up to file reports, they were sent away. Frequently when young girls came to report rapes, DNIC officers would hit on them for dates while taking their declarations. Other times, women reporting domestic violence incidents were berated by agents who suggested they deserved the husband's abuse.

Sometimes victims were given notes to deliver to their offending husbands, demanding their appearance at police headquarters. Others were just turned away.

When victims came to us, we comforted them, prayed with them, provided them with the things they needed in the moment, whether it was food, medical attention, diapers, or bottles for their baby, and walked them through the process while providing a calm and safe environment.

But we also advocated for their cases. We kept tabs on the DNIC to ensure they completed the required steps in the process. When they refused to cooperate, or gave us trouble, we went to their superior, or the colonel in charge, to pressure them into doing their jobs.

An example of these challenges came to our attention one late afternoon while returning from a mission in Orica, a mountain community two hours from Talanga. A *transito* officer (traffic police) called me from his post at the entrance to Talanga.

"Gracie, I need your help," he said. "There's a pregnant lady here with bruises all over her. She asked me to stop cars and ask who was driving past the Orica exit so she could hitch a ride home since there are no more buses today. I asked her why she was traveling alone and so late, and she said she had gone to the DNIC because her husband beat her, but they refused to help her."

"We are actually returning from Orica right now," I told him. "We should be passing your post in about ten minutes. Keep her there so we can speak to her."

This case was prior to Colonel O's arrival on the scene, and we had widespread support and cooperation from officers who embraced the program.

I really loved how the good officers embraced the work. Many called me late at night to ask for advice or help. I loved teaching them, counseling them, watching the people in the villages see the transformation of these officers. Many of the police officers began to see themselves as protectors of the helpless. The people in the villages could see this transformation and began to trust the police. They began to believe there was hope in their cases. It was amazing.

Years later I can still see the young, pregnant woman standing at the post as we pulled up in the truck. The sun was dipping low in the sky and the shadows were long. Her stomach protruded from her flower-patterned, cotton dress as she raised her hand to shade her eyes from the low sun's glare. There were bruises on her face, along her arms, and on her legs below the hem of the dress down to her feet, which were clad in cheap, purple flip-flops.

She and the officer approached the window on the passenger's side of our truck to speak with me. I listened as they both told me how she had traveled for hours from Orica, sometimes walking the dusty, dirt road, grabbing a bus when she could, and then hitchhiking the rest of the way. She said when she arrived at the police station, the female DNIC officer yelled at her, saying she was supposed to file the report in Orica and told her to go home.

The bruised and pregnant woman, who had been viciously and verbally attacked by the DNIC officer, walked two miles to the entrance of Talanga and asked transit police to help her hitchhike back to Orica. There were no buses at that time of day, and the road she had to take was dangerous at any time, nevermind the night hours when she would have had to travel the road alone. Then, of course, if she arrived home safely, she would have to face her husband and explain where she had been all day.

I was furious. The law clearly stated victims could place their report at any police station, and the officers were to remit their cases to the authorities with jurisdiction over them. She climbed into the back seat of our truck, and I thanked the officer for doing such a good job in recognizing a problem and assisting a helpless woman.

When we pulled into a space in front of the station, the DNIC officer was sitting on the front porch on one of the benches, her legs stretched out in front of her as she fiddled with her cellphone. We approached Agent Ara, who looked up and frowned when she saw who accompanied us.

"We have a case," I said, standing in front of her. "We need to do a domestic violence report."

She didn't look up and continued tapping on her phone.

"I already told her she has to report it in Orica. This isn't the jurisdiction for her case," Agent Ara said in an annoyed tone as she waved her arm toward the pregnant woman.

Everyone on and around the porch grew silent, watching us.

"I understand what you told her," I said, "but the law says she can report anywhere and then we remit it to the appropriate authorities."

Agent Ara exploded as she jumped out of her seat.

"Who are you to tell me what to do? She must report it in Orica. It isn't my jurisdiction."

She gestured toward the pregnant woman and began to berate her.

"I told you to go back home and report it there to the police or the judge!" she continued, using many other words I cannot repeat here, insulting the woman in front of everyone.

The pregnant woman began to cry. I took her arm, led her to the other bench, and sat her down, telling her it would be okay. Furious, I turned to Agent Ara.

"You are revictimizing this poor woman! Not only is it a violation of law for you to refuse to help her, but you also turned a pregnant woman out into the street without any humanity at an hour she could not safely get back home. You know we have a refuge right there!"

I turned and pointed at the lavender-colored building across the street. "Just thirty feet from your office door there!" I turned back to Ara and pointed at the door behind her in reception. "You know we can care for her throughout the night and get her safely home tomorrow."

At that time we were building our refuge at our ministry in La Ermita. Until the construction was finished, we had rented a space across the street from the police in which victims could stay if needed.

Agent Ara and I argued for several minutes. I was disgusted by her lack of empathy for this woman. She refused to do her job and threw the woman out into the street without worrying what might happen to her. She had no excuse, such as being busy with another case. She wasn't doing anything except sitting on the porch playing on her cellphone.

These are the moments when God shows up—sometimes in a grand manner. There were maybe twenty people on and around the entrance to the police station and other officers were watching from reception.

"It's not my job," Agent Ara shouted. "She has to file it in Orica."

"Ara, the law requires any officer or agent to take the case wherever the victim presents to file it."

Around and around we went.

I asked her where her superior was, and she said the inspector was off. Frustrated, I pulled out my cellphone, called Colonel Antonio, and he answered on the second ring.

"Good evening, *Jefe*," I said. "I am sorry to bother you at this hour, but I need your help. We have a seven-month pregnant, domestic violence victim here and agent Ara is refusing to take her report because the woman came from Orica. She threw her out in the street to walk home. She knows we have the refuge right here and neglected to let the victim know there was additional help."

Colonel Antonio asked me a few more details.

"Yes, sir," I replied. "I do know that it is jurisdiction of Orica, but Ara can take the report, have the forensic doctor review the woman's wounds, especially since she is so far advanced in her pregnancy. We can admit her to our refuge for the night and tomorrow we can pay the bus fare for a safe journey home. She can take the documents with her to give to the authorities there. I need to pass the phone to Agent Ara, so you can talk with her."

"That won't be necessary," he replied.

He was in his office upstairs and would be coming down to speak with us directly. I had thought he had left for the evening as was his usual routine to visit people and have dinner away from the police station.

I looked directly at agent Ara.

"He is on his way down," I told her.

Colonel Antonio pushed through the swinging door at the back of the *guardia* and came out onto the porch with his customary swagger of authority. He was the best commander we had worked with and had brought us to a 90 percent reporting rate of special victims with a 71 percent closure rate on the cases. That was unheard of in Honduras, where nationally the reporting rate is 30 percent and the closure rate an abysmal 1-4 percent.

He walked over to the woman and asked her what happened. She began crying the minute he gently touched her shoulder and recounted the story of her long and arduous journey to arrive at the police seeking help.

"My husband beat me; kicked me in the stomach," she said through sobs as she rubbed her baby bump. "I am afraid he hurt the baby. I came for help and she yelled at me and sent me away!" The woman pointed at Agent Ara as she spoke. "I walked to the transit post to get a ride and the officer called Gracie."

She told him how we brought her back and agent Ara continued to publicly berate her and again refused to help.

The colonel gently examined the many bruises on her arms and legs, as well as the angry, red finger marks around her neck. He then turned to Agent Ara. He walked over to the other side of the porch where the offending agent was standing. Agent Ara jumped at attention and saluted him.

"You will take this woman's report," Colonel Antonio said, his voice fierce and firm. "You will send her to Dr. Ferrera's clinic for a forensic exam, and you will send the reports with her on the bus tomorrow, so she can give them to the judge there."

"Yes sir!" she replied.

The colonel also told her to never refuse to take a report again and that she needed to learn to treat victims with respect.

His words were firm and clear, and loud enough to be heard by the now large crowd of silent onlookers. As the colonel spoke, agent Ara threw several furtive glances in my direction to let me know she was not pleased with me.

That night after the report and declaration were completed, we accompanied the woman to the forensic doctor, prayed with her, fed her, and comforted her. The woman who stayed with victims in our temporary refuge was called in, and she saw that the pregnant woman was safe through the night. The next morning we fed her breakfast, prayed with her again, gave her my contact information, and paid for her bus ticket home.

The judge in Orica received her case, held a hearing with the husband, issued a protection order, and removed the husband from her house. Two months later while I was doing an orientation with a mission team that had come to work with us, my cellphone rang. It was her. She was calling to thank us for our help and to tell me that the night before she had given birth to a healthy baby boy.

These are the moments in which God shows up. He brings rescue and imprints his love on the lives of those who suffer. But they are also moments that breed enemies. Agent Ara was lazy. She didn't want to do her job, and when we took measures to make her do it, she was publicly and dramatically reprimanded.

This happened over and over throughout the years, bringing us to a point in November 2009 in which the chief of the DNIC and Colonel Quintin, another good colonel who worked with us, called a meeting to discuss the problems. It was set for 9 a.m. on Monday, November 23, 2009.

The night before, the police and the DNIC had been doing *operativos* on the street. They stopped buses and vehicles, checked identifications and vehicle registrations, searched for weapons and drugs. In doing so they came upon a group of men in possession of various guns that were illegal for citizens to have, including AK-47s.

It was the week before the national elections for a new president, mayors and Congress, and many *operativos* were being carried out. In June 2009 the Supreme Court, Congress, the military, and the police had ousted President Mel Zelaya and put in an interim president. Many called it a coup; others called it a political crisis. For months there had been violence throughout the country.

I went to the office early that morning to prepare for the meeting. Colonel Quintin entered and asked me if the chief of the DNIC was ready for the meeting because he needed to go to Tegucigalpa for other meetings afterwards. I told him I could go check for him.

This is another moment forever ingrained into my brain. The office of the DNIC was a small room off the right side of the *guardia*, or reception area. As I walked in, DNIC agents were standing around as a few inspected the weapons they had decommissioned the night before. I don't believe I had ever seen so many high-caliber weapons in one place.

"Is your *jefe* here?" I asked.

Agent Elmer lowered the weapon he was inspecting and told me his boss would not be in the office that day.

"The colonel sent me," I said. "We have a meeting with your boss in five minutes and he wanted me to check on him."

All were silent, staring at me until someone said their boss was on his way.

"Let him know the colonel is waiting," I replied.

As I stepped into the *guardia* and pulled the door shut behind me, I heard someone inside shout "Gracie!" I turned, pushing the door open, and stepped around it to look inside and see what they wanted.

Another moment in my life that time froze.

I came eye to eye with Agent Elmer as he raised an AK-47 directly at me from behind a desk, staring at me through the scope, with his finger on the trigger. No one said a word. My heart stopped, but my mind raced. They were threatening me—all of them. No one outside could see what they were doing. Agent Elmer and I stood face-to-face with the business end of an AK-47 pointed in my face.

"What the hell are you doing raising a gun at me, threatening me?" I shouted so the officers and people in the *guardia* and on the porch could hear me.

"How dare you threaten me!" I continued, hoping there were others listening outside.

The DNIC agents all started laughing and someone said something to the effect that I couldn't handle a joke.

As I turned to leave, I shouted, "When your boss gets here, tell him to get to our meeting and don't you ever threaten me with a weapon again!"

I stepped out and slammed the door as hard as I could. My heart was pounding hard in my chest.

There was a sergeant sitting at the desk in the *guardia* outside the door.

"Are you alright?" he asked, his face filled with concern.

"Yes," I said. "Can you believe that they had the audacity to raise a gun at me as a threat because I have a meeting with their boss and the colonel about their negligence?"

He shook his head and told me to be careful. I went straight to the colonel's office.

When Agent Elmer raised the AK-47 at my face, I didn't know what to do. They were not visible from the *guardia*. I had to do something to let the people outside know what was going on inside. Otherwise it would be my word against theirs. I screamed at them, so those outside could hear what was going on inside the office.

Time after time and case after case, we fought with DNIC agents to do their jobs. Only one *fiscal* (prosecutor) and a judge fought with us through the years. The greatest challenge we faced was with the DNIC office.

There was also an incident that caused us problems with a driver and a secretary of the prosecutor's office.

On April 3, 2011, we received a thirteen-year-old girl named Oda in our refuge for temporary care. She arrived in the prosecutor's truck with Marco, the *fiscalia's* driver, and Sara, a female police officer. The girl was violent and tried to escape as they brought her in. Officer Sara said Oda had been difficult in the police station and should be considered a flight risk. The officer and driver were not friendly, nor were they kind with the girl at all.

When they left we sat down to speak with Oda and find out about her life. She told us that she previously lived with her mother and other people in a village named Rio Dulce and that her mother, who was in Spain with her new husband and child, had sent her to Irvine, California, with two other young cousins ages six and twelve when she was six years old. She said a man she did not know took them to Mexico then transferred them to a *coyote,* a human-trafficker, to deliver them to their grandparents in California.

Her grandmother and aunt, Oda said, were involved in prostitution in Los Angeles under the cover of a massage parlor. She said she had gone to high school but hated being there because of sexual abuse she suffered from her grandfather and because she didn't like being around the massage parlor (prostitution) business. Conflict arose as she grew older and her mother told her grandmother to send her back to Honduras. The girl told us that she had flown—without a passport and using only a birth certificate—from Los Angeles into Tegucigalpa, arriving at 8 a.m. the same day she came to our ministry.

I immediately knew something was wrong with her story. No flights arrive from the United States before eleven, and minors are not allowed to fly alone internationally, and nobody can board international flights without a passport.

I asked Oda if the authorities said anything to her when she arrived in Tegucigalpa. She said immigration officials held her for about ten minutes, but when she showed them her birth certificate they let her go. None of this made sense, either. Her unlikely story led me to believe Oda had been in the hands of not only human traffickers, but also sex traffickers.

Her birth certificate was old, faded, and marked by years of use. Only her mother was listed as a parent. No father was named. We asked about her father and if she had any family. She told us her "Aunt Roma," in Rio Dulce, would know where her family was located. She asked us to try to find her father and family because she did not want to go to IHNFA (*Instituto Hondureño de la Niñez y la Familia*), the government child-welfare institution whose orphanages were operated more like prisons than homes.

The following day she left for IHNFA. Marco, the prosecutor's driver, and the same female officer, Sara, were charged with taking Oda to the children's court judge in Tegucigalpa, who would then send her to IHNFA. The driver and officer didn't look pleased to be dealing with Oda again and discussed cuffing her for the ride since she had been such a problem the day before. Oda promised she would behave because I was going to look for her family. I hugged her tightly before she left, prayed over her, and promised I would look for her family.

That weekend I went to Rio Dulce, a village of about four hundred people five kilometers from our ministry at the intersection of our road and the road to Tegucigalpa. I met with Roma, the woman Oda said was her aunt. The houses of the people she mentioned were on the main road. Both had small businesses, one a small snack and food store, the other a billiards hall. I met with Roma and she told me she was not Oda's aunt. She said Oda's mother had come to the village years before, lived with a woman named Maria, and became pregnant a short time later.

I asked her if she knew Oda's father.

"There are three possibilities," Roma said, "but no one knows for sure. The first possibility is Maria's son, Will. There was also a man from El Salvador who dated her briefly, and then there was a man from Talanga who was murdered two years ago."

I was worried when Will's name came up because we had a case during 2009 where he was suspected to have impregnated a thirteen-year-old girl.

After speaking with Roma, I went to Maria's house, which was across the street from her home.

The first thing I perceived when I saw Maria was that she was guarded. She was friendly enough, but there was a sense in my spirit not to trust her. We had spoken before when her son had been suspected of having sex with a thirteen-year-old girl. I asked her if her son was Oda's father.

"It was about fourteen years ago when Oda's mother came to Rio Dulce," she said. "She was already pregnant when she arrived. Nobody knows who Oda's father is—except for her mother. They lived here for a bit and then her mother met a man, had a boy, and a year later the three of them moved to Spain, leaving Oda with me. A short time later, she told me to send Oda to her grandmother in the USA."

Maria explained that it was Oda's uncle, Alfredo, who took the three children to Mexico for their journey to America with a *coyote*. She said the uncle lived in Tegucigalpa.

"It was in February, almost two months ago, when Alfredo showed up at my house at nine in the morning without warning," Maria said. "He said Oda had arrived by plane at six or seven in the morning and he picked her up, brought her to me, and told me her mother wanted her here with me."

Alarm bells rang in my head. This story was getting weirder by the moment. Oda had told me she had arrived from the United States at 8 a.m. on the same day she was brought to our ministry. But Maria was saying the same man who took her and picked her up was Oda's uncle. The flight information and times of arrival in both stories didn't make sense either. Again, my mind was drifting toward the idea of traffickers. I had heard through informants that there was a sex-trafficking ring in Rio Dulce, but we were never able to figure out who were involved.

"When Oda arrived, she had two piercings in her mouth and a lot of makeup and sexy clothes," Maria said. "All she had for documentation was a birth certificate. She was aggressive and had a bad attitude with everyone. She didn't obey our rules and kept trying to go out to hang with men."

Maria explained that when Oda moved out to live with the daughter of another neighbor, Dora, that she went to the police to put in the report for a child at risk. It was then I realized who called the police to pick up Oda. The prosecutor hadn't told me. Another alarm bell rang as Dora was the mother of the pregnant girl suspected of having relations with Maria's son Will in 2009, two years prior.

We talked a few minutes longer and Maria gave me names and telephone numbers of Oda's family members. Then I left.

The case became more suspicious by the moment. I learned the DNIC had handled this case for more than a month without passing it to our special-victims office, and the only reason knowledge of the case came to me was because the prosecutor finally decided to have the police pick her up, so they could send her to IHNFA. We were having a great deal of problems with the DNIC not passing cases to our office.

During the next few days I began receiving calls and text messages from men saying they were Oda's cousins and they wanted to know where she was. I also received a strange message from Will asking for information on Oda. No women called, only men. I didn't give any of them information but said I would give their names and numbers to the authorities involved in her case.

A few days later I was at Casitas Kennedy, the IHNFA orphanage, in Tegucigalpa for a meeting over a child they were placing with us. I told the orphanage's director I had information for Oda, who had been admitted the week before, and I wanted to give it to her and to them, so they could work to find her family.

The director sent her assistant to look for the child's file and bring it to her office. The assistant returned with the log book, which notes when children enter and leave the facility. Oda's name was not in it. She had never been brought to IHNFA.

The director was concerned because the child had no family, her mother was in Spain, and there was no father on her birth certificate. I showed her my documents, which included the order from the prosecutor's office for the driver to take Oda to the children's court judge, who would then send her to Casitas Kennedy. My document included the time, date, and signature of the driver, Marco, who transported her.

The child was missing, according to the national child welfare office. The director asked me to investigate what happened after Oda left our ministry. I called my office and asked Karina, our advocate, to go to the prosecutor's office and find out what happened after Marco, the driver, and Sara, the female police officer, left the ministry with Oda.

Sometimes a simple question can blow up in your face and ignite a war.

Karina called the prosecutor's office and spoke with the secretary, then she called me a few minutes later.

"The copy of the remission to the judge was signed by the judge's secretary that Oda had been delivered to them that morning," Karina reported. "I asked the prosecutor's secretary what the judge did with Oda, but she didn't know. She said we would have to speak with Marco and Officer Sara."

The director of Casitas Kennedy ordered me to investigate and find out where Oda had gone. Procedure, by law, was for a minor without family to be delivered directly from the child court judge's office to IHNFA. The child court judge, upon receiving Oda, should have delivered her directly to Casitas Kennedy the same day.

The following day Karina called me and said she had called the prosecutor's office a second time to ask about Oda and spoke with the secretary again. We previously had problems with this woman. Her sister was married to a DNIC agent, and she had been giving us trouble for weeks.

"She [the prosecutor's office secretary] told me the judge gave Oda to her father," Karina reported. "They didn't need to send her to Casita's Kennedy."

"How is that possible, Karina, if there was no father on the birth certificate?" I asked.

"Gracie, I don't know," she replied. "I don't see how that is possible since no one knows who her father is, including Oda."

We personally knew the judges in the children's court and they would have had to do an extensive investigation, including communicating with Oda's mother in Spain, to find out who her father was. There wasn't time for that, and the court just doesn't give a child to anyone.

We continued to communicate with the prosecutor's office and each time we received a different answer. One story was that the judge gave Oda to Sara, the female police officer, who had brought her to the court, so she could take Oda to her father. Another story was that the judge gave Oda to Marco, the prosecutor's driver, because he was Oda's father.

Both stories were lies. The following day Officer Sara approached Karina in the courtyard of the police station outside our office and began insulting her in an aggressive manner.

"You shouldn't be sticking your nose where it doesn't belong," Sara told Karina. "I'm being told by people in the prosecutor's office that you are looking into Oda and talking about me. The judge gave her to me and I gave her to her father!"

A sergeant heard the altercation, approached them, and asked them to take it somewhere else because a lot of people were listening to them.

Karina went back to work, ignoring the insults and threats Sara hurled at her. A short time later, Officer Sara passed our office and threatened to assault Karina.

"I have lots of friends in high places," Sara shouted at Karina. "And we have orders from Colonel O not to help you and not let anyone pass into the station to your office. You are nobody and soon you'll be out of here, and you can't do anything against me!"

To say Karina was a bit shaken, having been verbally assaulted in front of officers and civilians, was an understatement. I told her to go to Tegucigalpa the next day to internal affairs and file a report. A child was missing under strange circumstances involving the driver for the prosecutor's office and a police officer. We were ordered by IHNFA to investigate and the response to our investigation was this attack and more strange stories.

When Karina arrived at internal affairs, she had a pleasant surprise. The officer in charge happened to be *Inspectora*, the female inspector, who had previously been head of the DNIC when Colonel O was first assigned to Talanga. We discovered she had been assigned to Talanga undercover by the internal affairs department.

Nothing ever happened with our report to internal affairs. We filed a report with the children's court judge and IHNFA about Oda's disappearance, but nothing happened there either.

Three months later Karina called me from the office.

"I just received some intelligence that Oda is back in Rio Dulce and she is pregnant by Dora's son Will."

About two months later, late at night, the truck from the prosecutor's office appeared with a small child to put into our care for the night. I was shocked to see Oda sitting in the front passenger seat eating fried chicken with her belly full of baby. The driver was Marco, the same driver who had taken her to the judge the day she disappeared. He gave us the child he was bringing, and we filled out the paperwork while Oda sat happily in the front seat. She was "hanging out" with the driver while he did his work late at night.

But the story didn't end there. In early 2012 a secretary for the children's court showed up at our door to ask about a twelve-year-old girl who was in our children's home. I didn't recognize the name. She gave me the date of the child's arrival, and I looked in our log book. The girl had been with us one night. The following day the driver for the prosecutor's office had signed documents that he had taken her to the children's court judge.

However, according to the secretary of the children's court, the girl never arrived. I told her about Oda's case and showed her the documents I had on her case. She telephoned her office and had someone investigate the files. It turns out that both girls' files arrived at the court, but neither of the girls were delivered to them. Both girls had left our ministry in the prosecutor's office vehicle with their driver, but they never arrived at the court. We knew where Oda was, but the other? No one ever found her.

The more we investigated this situation, the more grief and attacks we suffered. Marco is still working for the prosecutor's office.

No one would help us. Usually we went to the colonel to help, but at that time, the commander was Colonel O, and he was doing everything he could to sabotage our work and get us out of there.

A short time later, in prayer, the Lord told me the office for victims would be closed by October 31, 2011. Everything inside me screamed, "No! That could not happen!" We had worked so hard for so long and had done such a good job. In my mind, the Lord was warning me of a possibility. It couldn't be true. There must be something we could do. We had to stand and keep fighting.

Then things went from bad to worse.

CHAPTER TWELVE

THE END OF THE BEGINNING
(OF EVERYTHING)

*"Whatever happens, conduct yourselves in a manner worthy
of the gospel of Christ . . . stand firm . . . without being
frightened in any way by those who oppose you. This is a
sign to them that they will be destroyed, but that you will be
saved—and that by God."*
Philippians 1:27–28 (NIV)

April through November 2011 were some of the most difficult months of my life. Colonel O was intensifying his attacks and sabotage, the DNIC agents were not doing their work and were fighting us on every corner. It was all we could do to hang on.

After Holy Week 2010, Karina told me Colonel O came to our office several times saying he was single with lots of money and in love with her. He went into detail about his alleged wealth, including that he has three houses, one worth more than a million dollars. She told him she was not interested and noted she had a husband who was an officer under his command.

"I can assign your husband far from Talanga," Colonel O told her. "He would be out of our way."

Karina told me she sensed he was trying to force her to go out with him on a date, and if she didn't, he alleged he was not going to support our work or would force us out.

She said she conceded to his dinner date requests to comply with his threats. He took her to several places where alcoholic beverages flowed throughout the night. To protect herself from his advances, she always made sure the *Inspectora*, the head of the DNIC went with her. She did not feel safe to be alone with him.

Ranking officers and police informed me that Colonel O was angry and was fabricating a plan to evict our program from his headquarters. The *Inspectora*, head of the DNIC, told me she had problems with him too. She said she shared my annual report with him, so he could understand our work, but he tossed it in the trash and told her he wasn't interested.

During April 2010, a general, the *Inspectora's* superior, came from Tegucigalpa to carry out an inspection and Colonel O refused to furnish the customary lunch. The *Inspectora* came to me for help, and I paid for her and her boss' lunch from my meeting budget. I also joined them for lunch and spoke with the general about our work. Colonel O refused to eat with them because I provided the visiting general's lunch he would not.

Police officers began to tell us that Colonel O claimed he had all the DNIC agents and prosecutors set against me personally. He claimed he had documentation of illegal activities I had committed, such as illegally ordering the arrest or detention of a person. We were informed that Colonel O told others he was going to do whatever he could to throw us out in the street.

In addition, several officers, including the *Inspectora*, told me Colonel O was telling people I was an FBI spy, had a salary of $10,000 per month, and I received $500 for each case we handled. He alluded that the United States government was paying me to be a spy. All fabricated accusations.

The situation was overwhelming. I felt like I was walking through chest-deep mud to move forward. I could not understand why so much time and effort were being wasted on nonsense when it all could have been put toward helping people.

Many nights I sat on my couch and cried. I wanted to surrender. It was too hard. Why were we here if they didn't want us? The people who were supposed to be helping to serve victims were the same people sabotaging the work.

But everyone knew the truth; everyone knew we were unjustly attacked. I don't know how many times someone gave me a hug and whispered "Hang in there," or "We understand." It was those moments and the moments when victims hugged us and thanked us for helping them get justice, that gave us hope.

I had to believe we could work it out. I had to believe there was some way to get Colonel O to understand that we were there to help him, not fight him. I sought him out several times to explain our work, find out what his issues with us were, and seek a way to resolve them.

Invariably, he either ignored me or told me he did not have time. He almost never spoke to me and he sent his responses to my petitions through Karina.

During May 2010, I ran into Colonel O in the courtyard at the headquarters and asked him about a work meeting.

"I don't have time for a meeting with you," he said. "I want you to fix your office door, making it a glass door like the others. You need to paint your office and fix the windows. There is also water coming in through the wall when it rains so you need to fix that too."

There was nothing wrong with our door or the windows; he just wanted a different style. And the office had recently been painted. The leaky wall, however, was part of the physical structure of the headquarters and the colonel's responsibility.

"These things are not my responsibility," I said. "They are yours because they pertain to the physical structure of the police headquarters."

He responded with theatrical threats in front of other police officers.

"I want your space for something else. If you don't do the remodeling I demand, I will kick you out onto the street."

Later that day he came into the office and told Karina the same thing.

That night, without my knowledge, he once again coerced Karina to go out with him for dinner and drinks. The following morning she related to me an incident the night before when the colonel was talking to others.

"If anyone goes against me," he said, holding up his hand, putting his forefinger on his thumb, gesturing as though he was squashing something between his fingers, "they won't be around for long."

Karina was concerned. She said the evil she saw in Colonel O's eyes led her to believe it was more than just talk; he was going to take action against me.

"It was a threat," Karina insisted. "Don't ever tell him, or anyone, where you are going, or when, or anything about your schedule. I feel it in my bones. You are in grave danger with this guy."

During this time I met with our supporting generals in Tegucigalpa to discuss the situation with the colonel, which had digressed from mere annoyances and threats to actual actions. The DNIC office had begun blocking access of victims to our office.

For example, a sergeant secretly informed us a woman entered the headquarters seeking assistance from our office. A female DNIC agent told her I was not in the office that day, and our advocate could not attend her because she didn't speak Spanish—an outright lie. The victim tried to make her report with the agent, but she refused to take it and sent the victim away.

The *Inspectora*, who had been an internal-affairs plant investigating what was going on in Talanga, had been moved to Tegucigalpa in June 2010. Her replacement came to our office to interrogate Karina about me. Repeating the lies Colonel O had been spreading about me being an FBI spy, he pressed her for information about my personal life and schedule . . . Where did I go every day? . . . What did I do? . . . How did I get my money? . . . Who paid me?

Previously we had been given access to the denuncia book (case log) in the DNIC each morning so we could find special crimes cases that had not passed to our office, seek out the victims, and help them. Once this new DNIC chief took command, our access was denied. Rumors around the station were that we were looking for drug cases in the book and reporting them to the DEA because we were spies.

Several policemen pulled me aside and said the colonel was telling the police during their formations that we did not pay for the office space, or for utilities, and that we should be paying them something. The officer said he was always trashing us.

We allowed another children's home the use of our refuge facility in La Ermita as a safe and neutral spot for family visits. During a family visitation day in January 2011, one of the visiting mothers, a Talanga resident, was overheard telling other parents that she has friends in the DNIC who told her not only the lie that I was an FBI spy, but also that it was all part of a diabolical plan to take Honduran children to the United States.

Over and over we received similar reports. It was as though Colonel O was working every angle he could to slander and destroy us.

One evening during March 2011, a friend, who was one of the ranking officers at the station, sought me out to tell me an order had come from Colonel O that we were to evacuate our office space inside the courtyard. The location, which had its own bathroom, was ideal because it ensured privacy for the victims. Instead, we were being ordered to move to a public space in the reception area.

The official's face was filled with embarrassment. He had been charged by Colonel O, who had left for the weekend, to deliver me the order. He wasn't pleased about it. I told him I didn't believe we would be moving and would get back to him later. I immediately called General Cesar in the capital, filling him in on the situation. He ordered me not to move the office.

Returning to the front porch, where I found the official sitting on the bench, I put my hand on his shoulder and gently told him we would not be moving. He jumped to his feet, worry lines filling his face.

"But he ordered you to move tonight," he said.

"I know," I replied. "But the law requires victims to have privacy. This office here has no door, is without electricity or plugs for our computers, and is right at the entrance where everyone can hear what is going on inside the office. We will not be moving."

"But the colonel will be angry," the official said. "He ordered me to move you."

I smiled at him.

"Don't you worry a thing," I said as I put my hand on his chest over his badge and leaned in to softly speak into his ear. "You did your job and informed me. Your order was to deliver the message, not to physically move our office. I answered you, saying we would not move. The general, who has more power than Colonel O does, told me to stay. They will handle it."

I hugged him and left.

And they did. A day or two later, one of the highest-ranking officials in the capital appeared at the headquarters. I was at court with a victim at the time, but informants within the headquarters told me the general told Colonel O, "Don't touch the *gringa*."

We did not move the office and Colonel O didn't like it. His actions became more fervent. We were told he ordered all police officers not to allow victims to pass through reception to our office. Officers who disobeyed would be punished. On some days the colonel sat in a chair in the reception for hours to make sure the order was enforced.

One day a rape victim approached the front desk while Colonel O was sitting in a chair to the side. She asked for Karina but was told she wasn't in the office that day. The woman called Karina and discovered she was indeed in the office. The woman told her she had gone to the forensic doctor for her evaluation and found out he wouldn't be available until the next day. She needed bus money to get home and come back. Karina left the headquarters and secretly met the woman at the courthouse to give her bus money.

The secretaries in other offices were ordered not to visit our office. They were prohibited from speaking with Karina or using our office bathroom. DNIC agents were ordered not to tell victims of the assistance we provided or inform our office of any victims who filed cases.

It was as though Colonel O was trying to use brute force to remove us. Everyone was uncomfortable. If our friends within the police spoke to us, they risked punishment from the colonel.

At times when we encountered victims in front of the headquarters, DNIC agents told us we were prohibited from speaking to them or lending them assistance by order of the prosecutor's office. I spoke with the head of the prosecutor's office, a good friend of ours and woman who fights for justice in each case she receives. She denied issuing any such order. She suggested the fabrications were coming from the colonel and the DNIC.

The situation created confusion among the public. They heard us on the radio show talking about our work, but when they went to the headquarters to ask for our help, they were told the office didn't exist. One victim who knew we were there and tried to pass through to our office was physically blocked by a DNIC agent. He also snatched her copy of her police report out of her hands to prevent her from sharing it with us. The whole thing was insane.

One of the reasons the DNIC agents were so eager to cooperate with the colonel's efforts to get rid of us is that not only did they dump cases, but they also extorted victims and their families. A father whose child was missing was told by agents that if he paid for the gasoline and the food they needed while searching for his daughter, they would look for his child. If the father was unable to pay, no search was mounted.

In another case, DNIC agents needed documents from Tegucigalpa for a case. They made the victim's family cover their gas and food for the trip. On Monday they told the family they needed more money to go back to the capital because when they went, on Saturday, the offices were closed.

I don't believe they ever went. Instead of going, they just pocketed the money. The DNIC agents were not happy with us for telling victims or their families it was illegal to give them money to work cases.

Sabotage was the game they were playing. One day a DNIC agent came into our office when Karina was momentarily away and installed a virus on our computer, causing us to lose many of our files. Another time they borrowed our USB to put one of their files on it, so Karina could print it for them because there was no ink in their printer.

Instead of coming back with our USB, they took it to Colonel O and looked through all our files and reports. Some were confidential reports to officials in the capital about the abuse we suffered from Colonel O and the negligence and corruption of the officials in the DNIC in Talanga.

During the end of July 2011, I was visiting Hospital Escuela, the public hospital in Tegucigalpa, for a case involving a child. Karina called me to report on cases that had come in the night before. She informed me that she had received information from an informant about a case that had happened in Guaimaca, a town about thirty-five minutes north of Talanga, four days prior.

A minor had been attacked, raped and almost killed by a machete-wielding assailant. The attacker had been detained, but DNIC agents released him without carrying out an investigation, and citizens were outraged by their negligence. Karina said the victim was supposedly still in Hospital Escuela and she gave me his name.

Being a public and government-run hospital, there was a DNIC office on the main floor to handle the shootings, rapes, and other criminal cases that came in with patients. I went there for help in finding the child. The DNIC officers at Hospital Escuela were always supportive, and they readily consulted their book.

We found his name in the book and the note said Mark had been admitted four days earlier for "rape, serious injury, and attempted murder by machete," but strangely it listed him not as a child, but as an adult who was mentally disabled.

I called Marlene Reyes, the representative of the Municipal Women's Office of Guaimaca who represented our office in that town. She filled me in on the case.

"The twenty-two-year-old mentally disabled Mark was raped by a known man who attacked him with a machete. Mark was rescued by a couple who were walking by and heard his screams for help," she said. "They took him in a private car to the Guaimaca Baptist Hospital, where he received medical attention.

"It was a zoo at the hospital," Marlen exclaimed. "Local media and the Guaimaca police arrived at the hospital. Inspector Tomas, acting commander of the Guaimaca police station, took statements and told the couple he was going to report the case to the regional headquarters in Talanga. Then the couple took Mark in a private car to Hospital Escuela in Tegucigalpa because he was going to die if he did not go immediately and there was no ambulance available."

"What about the guy who attacked him? Do they have him?" I asked.

"The next day, the *auxiliadoras* [civilian auxiliaries] captured him," she said. "They turned him in to the Guaimaca police, who delivered him to the DNIC agents in Talanga."

"It's been four days, is the man still in jail?" I asked her.

"You won't believe this. The next day the DNIC agents let him go!" Marlen said, her voice angry.

"Why did they do that?" I asked. "He practically killed the boy and cut his arm off! And there are witnesses to what happened too."

"The DNIC agents said they had no choice because no one showed up to file a *denuncia* [criminal complaint]," she said. "And until someone does, they can't do a thing."

I was livid. Although not a minor, the victim was disabled, and therefore entitled to special protection under the law. In special-victims' cases the government must act on what is called *oficio,* meaning they do not need a formal complaint to investigate. The disabled young man was taken to Tegucigalpa—in a car, not an ambulance—to save his life, and because he wasn't present to file the report, the DNIC let his alleged attacker go free and did nothing to investigate the case.

They should have traveled to Tegucigalpa to interview Mark and his rescuers, or called DNIC agents at the hospital and had them do it, and then have them pass on the information. It was another instance of the passive laziness of officials, something we encountered nearly every day. If the case didn't come to them, or it didn't pique their interest, they did nothing.

Unfortunately I was pressured for time and could not go see Mark or the couple caring for him. But I did ask the DNIC agents in the hospital to check on them and call me later, so we could follow up on the case. I called Karina and asked her to go back to the DNIC office and find out what they are doing on the case, inform them of where the victim was, and give them a push. Going to Colonel O was out of the question. He was obstructing and sabotaging everything we did.

Karina called me later to report that DNIC agents in Talanga refused to work the case, refused to call the hospital, and continued to maintain that they couldn't do anything until a formal complaint was received.

I was busy at the time working with top officials at Casamata, the national police headquarters, on a proposal for a grant from SICA (*Sistema de Integración Centroamericana*) to combat violence in Honduras. Some $400 million was being offered to Latin America by the international community to address the region's violence problem. All week I had been traveling to and from the capital to participate in these daylong meetings.

The next morning on my way into the capital, I called Karina and asked her to check again with Talanga's DNIC agents about them working on the case. I told her I had not heard anything from the DNIC in the hospital and would call them to make sure someone was working the case. However, because officers in the hospital unit are rotated every day, those working that day knew nothing about the case.

Karina called me that afternoon while I was on a coffee break with the generals to tell me the Talanga DNIC had told her again they would do nothing until a formal complaint was lodged. She had also received a phone call from an informant in Guaimaca who was indignant about the negligence of this case. The informant gave us the name and phone number of the couple who rescued Mark and now were taking care of him at Hospital Escuela.

I was exasperated. A twenty-two-year-old, mentally handicapped man had been brutally attacked, raped, and nearly hacked to death. Two Samaritans had saved him, and the community and local authorities had joined forces to capture his assailant. Then investigative authorities, who didn't care about this young man fighting for his life in the hospital, let the assailant go and refused to work the case.

The coffee break was over, and the meeting was beginning again. I told General Cesar I had to deal with something urgent and would be back in with them after I made another telephone call.

"Is there a problem?" he asked.

I told him it was the same problem we always had and would fill him in after the meeting was over. Then I excused myself and went out into the hallway to call the couple caring for Mark in the hospital.

The couple told me the same story. The authorities were not doing anything, and they could not leave the hospital to go to Talanga and file a formal complaint because Mark, who was valiantly fighting for his life, needed their attention. I asked them to go the DNIC in the hospital and file the complaint with them. The next day, after my meeting was over, I could pick up the report and take it to the DNIC in Talanga. They said they would file the complaint. I returned to the meeting.

The couple called me about a half an hour later, and I had to leave the meeting to go back into the hallway to speak with them. The DNIC agent at the hospital wanted to speak with me. He said his office could not take the complaint at the hospital and the couple had to go to the Metro 1 police station or to Talanga to file the report.

After I told the couple I would see what I could do, I ended the call, leaned against the wall, and silently cried. I felt alone in that moment, and unable to fight any more.

We were going around in circles. Nobody wanted to do their job. Nobody cared about this young man. Everyone had an excuse as to why they couldn't do what the law required them to do. I was so tired of fighting and tired of pushing. It felt as though no matter how hard we tried, we made no progress. Everything was going backward, not forward.

I felt hard-pressed on all sides, abandoned, and knocked down. This did not feel like a light and momentary affliction. I was losing heart; despair was seeping into my soul. I was lost and didn't know what to do.

As I wiped away tears with my sleeve, I saw General Cesar and the others through the glass, working on the proposal. They were so hopeful.

I loved the people in that group. We had worked together for many years and had many successes. All of them were strong Christians, including the general. I took a deep breath, finished wiping away my tears, and reentered the meeting.

When the meeting was over, and everyone was packing up their files and preparing to leave, General Cesar pulled me aside. He had the gentlest, but firm and strong, face I have ever seen.

"Tell me what is going on," he said. "I can tell you have been upset for the last few hours. Things in Talanga going bad?"

An ocean of tears threatened to escape my eyes and fall down my face. I couldn't speak, but I nodded. He took me down the hall into his office, led me to a sofa and handed me a box of tissues from the shelf. He gave me time to control my emotions and walked around behind his desk and sat in his chair, waiting for me to speak.

I shared with him the problems we were having in Talanga, including Colonel O sabotaging and blocking our work, and the DNIC agents not doing their work. I outlined the details and frustrations of the Guaimaca case we were currently trying to get the authorities to investigate.

"I feel like I am all alone, fighting against a river of hate and sabotage," I told him. "I can't do this much longer. Not with the way things are."

There are times in life when God blesses us with angels. And moments when life is too hard, too difficult and too impossible, that someone appears by your side to bring you hope and peace.

I remember the day I met this general. It was the celebration of the first year of our office in Talanga, and he had come to attend the ceremony. He was happy, bubbly, and funny. He was proud to love the Lord. We became great friends that day.

That night, as I sat in his office, broken and dejected, he became the angel God had sent to give me hope.

He told me DNIC agents are required to investigate such cases by *oficio,* without a formal complaint. He would ensure they investigated the Guaimaca case.

"Go to the hospital and talk to the couple caring for Mark," he told me. "Take their information and declarations. Get one from Mark if you can. Take pictures of Mark and his injuries, and then go back to Talanga and put in the formal report yourself. As chief of special crimes, and because this is a special crime, by law, you can put in the report. Then they will have to do their work."

He prayed with me right there in his office in national police headquarters. I left for the hospital with a glimmer of hope in my heart, a little less broken than the moment I entered his office an hour before.

A half hour later I walked into Mark's fifth-floor hospital room. I was shocked by his condition. Although twenty-two, he was the size of a young boy about twelve, no doubt because of malnourishment, with the mentality of a six-year-old boy. He lay on his back on a brightly colored and patterned sheet.

As he turned in my direction, his eyes filled with joy when I called his name and greeted him. There was no smile because the machete attack had cut the left side of his face from the corner of his mouth to his ear. Red, angry stitches lined the wound on the side of his face.

He was dressed only in a pair of Spiderman underwear underneath a sheet pulled up to his waist. His right arm ended in a bandage just below his elbow. The rest had been chopped off by the machete. His left shoulder was heavily bandaged. He had almost lost that arm from a deep machete cut, but the surgeons had saved it.

The couple who had rescued him stood by his bed. Although we had only spoken on the telephone, it felt as though we had known each other for years. They greeted me with hugs and offered me the only chair available in the room. I told them I would stand.

They, too, were angels . . . sent by God to save Mark. They never had met him before hearing his screams, but they had risked their lives to save his life by chasing off his armed attacker. They had taken him to the local hospital, made the two-hour trip to the capital city with him in their own car to again save his life because there was no ambulance. Now they had been with him in the hospital for a week assuring he received the care he needed. It was pure joy for me to see such care and sacrifice after my week of fruitless struggle to help Mark.

I took their and Mark's information then took photos of Mark and his injuries. I spoke with the nurses who had been caring for him. Everyone shared their frustrations with the authorities' negligence. I shared mine, and I told them a general was helping us. There would be justice for Mark.

Just before I prepared to leave, we joined hands over Mark's bed and prayed. We prayed for Mark's healing and well-being, for the authorities to do their work and for God to bring justice. When the amen was said, I sensed in my spirit that even though the general instructed me to file the formal complaint in Talanga, agents there would not allow me to do so. I quickly and silently prayed to God for guidance on what to do.

I felt a whisper of a name and knew exactly what to do.

After we had opened our first special-victims office in Talanga in 2006, the government opened one in Tegucigalpa. Officials wanted me to head it up, too, but with the capital city having close to a million people, I felt that was a monster I would be unable to tackle. Instead, they named an amazing woman, Inspector Fatima, to head the Tegucigalpa office. She and I worked many cases together, and I was greatly impressed that her unit's resolution rate of cases reached 90 percent in comparison to my office's lower, but also impressive, 70 percent rate.

It was her name I heard God whisper. I pulled out my cellphone and speed-dialed her number.

"Fatima," I said when she answered. "I need your help."

Inspector Fatima appeared at Mark's bedside in fewer than twenty minutes with two members of her team. After one look at Mark, five minutes listening to our story, and a quick call to the general, her team was working the case at full speed.

She called the prosecutor on duty that night in Tegucigalpa, raised the formal complaint by telephone, ordered her agents to take full declarations and formal statements from Mark and the couple who had rescued him.

"Where is his arm?" Inspector Fatima asked.

"It was cut off," I answered.

"But it is evidence," she said. "Where is it? We have to find it."

We both looked at the couple and they shrugged. We called in the nurse and asked her what the doctor did with the arm that had been cut off.

"I don't know," the nurse said. "They usually just throw that stuff in the trash after surgery."

We looked at each other and shook our heads. The stupidity and frustration of it all. But in the end, the absence of the arm was just as much evidence as its presence in a bag.

Inspector Fatima called and spoke with Inspector Tomas in Guaimaca who had handled Mark's case the day of the attack. He was another official who always was helpful to us. He shared with her all the details of the day of the crime, and how they had arrested the assailant. He expressed frustration with the Talanga DNIC agents for letting the suspect go.

"It is like the DNIC is undoing our good work. The people in Guaimaca are furious," he said. "This case and complaints about the DNIC in Talanga are all over the local television and radio news stations every night."

Inspector Fatima told her men to take my declaration on the negligence of the DNIC agents in Talanga. That same night, just before midnight, Mark was examined by the forensic doctor on duty and his report was completed and submitted to the prosecutor's office.

When Inspector Fatima sent me home, she told me I should rest because she would take care of everything, including an official report on the outright negligence of the DNIC agents in Talanga. I went home that night with hope for the first time in a long time.

God was moving. I wasn't alone in this fight.

The next morning, the last day of meetings in the national police headquarters over the proposal, General Cesar asked me how it went the night before. I told him Inspector Fatima came and took care of everything. He was pleased.

About twenty-four hours later, Inspector Fatima called to say her team had completed the procedures in Mark's case and they had submitted the case to the prosecutor. She was waiting for an arrest warrant for the assailant as well as a search warrant of his home.

Less than twenty-hours later, on Sunday morning, Inspector Fatima called to say she was sending a special team from Tegucigalpa to Guaimaca to find and arrest Mark's assailant. I kept in touch with the team throughout the day by phone and fed them lunch. At 4 p.m. Mark's assailant was captured and turned over to the Talanga prosecutor's office and the Talanga police station.

Over the course of fifty hours, Inspector Fatima and her Tegucigalpa team did all the work that the DNIC agents in Talanga refused to carry out in eight days. The assailant was sentenced to prison in the Talanga criminal court a few days later.

This was a case of complete negligence on the part of the Talanga DNIC, but also raised questions about Colonel O, who did nothing in the case. The case had been reported to him by Inspector Tomas the day of the attack. Colonel O was informed of the assailant's arrest the following day and again when the assailant was freed by the DNIC.

In addition, every day the Guaimaca media pestered Colonel O, asking why no one was doing anything about the case.

"I did not command the DNIC to do anything in this case because it isn't my obligation." Colonel O replied to their queries. "It is their responsibility, not mine."

He wasn't happy with us and didn't like that we went around him by reaching out to a superior of his and having a team from Tegucigalpa handle the case. Our victory fueled his hatred for us and gave further impetus to his campaign to oust us.

What he didn't know was General Cesar in Tegucigalpa had ordered me to write a report on every open case we had and to explain why they remained open. He wanted to know who was negligent and corrupt. He wanted every detail, even if it included the handiwork of Colonel O.

For the following two weeks I spent my time combing through the case files and our notes. I put together a report that I hoped would bring us the assistance we needed to continue the work without being sabotaged, attacked, and in fear for our lives.

Those eighteen months or so that Colonel O was chief in Talanga were something one might see in a movie.

Every day presented more obstacles. But the case of Mark, the raped and disfigured, mentally-challenged boy the DNIC agents refused to help, presented a ray of hope. I believed when the general told me to submit a report telling everything, that things would get better.

I spent the end of July and beginning of August 2011 working on the report. I submitted it to the general, along with copies to the Honduran national minister of security, minister of the national institute for women, and the head of the Honduran human rights office, among other leaders. During 2013 I also gave a copy to an official at the United States Embassy during a meeting on a case we had involving an American.

It was a bold act. I had put everything on the line, revealed everything, including evidence of witness tampering, agents falsifying documents, and other acts of negligence and corruption. The good police officers were terrified for us. Karina was terrified. I admit that I, too, was terrified.

When anyone takes a stand for anything in Honduras, the response is usually assassination.

It was late 2011 and we had been fighting for our lives for a year and a half.

God had to do something.

A lot of time was spent in prayer during those days. No one spoke of the report. The general said he had it and was working on it.

Ministry is not easy, and when you get into the devil's face, it can get downright ugly and difficult. Our justice ministry is probably one of the most powerful ministries I have ever seen or had the privilege to serve in. What greater work is there than to rescue those in hopeless and dangerous situations, help heal their wounds, save their lives, save their souls, and empower them to rise out of the ashes?

I have had to cling desperately to 2 Corinthians 4:1 (NIV): "Therefore, since through God's mercy we have this ministry, we do not lose heart."

When we began the victims office and ministry, we started with the knowledge that Honduras was one of the most violent countries on Earth. Women, children, the handicapped, and the elderly were targets for abuse, rape, murder, kidnapping, and authorities were hard-pressed to combat this violence against these vulnerable groups.

But our success in helping victims and completing our work was falling behind because corrupt and negligent officials were blocking victims' access to us.

"So justice is driven back, and righteousness stands at a distance; truth has stumbled in the streets, honesty cannot enter. Truth is nowhere to be found, and whoever shuns evil becomes a prey. The Lord looked and was displeased that there was no justice. He saw there was no one, <u>he was appalled that there was no one to intervene</u>." (Isa. 59:14–16 NIV)

We created a Christ-based program in response to the violence that required the collaboration of all government agencies and the people. The project was a great success. In a country where only a small percentage of people report the crimes because they believe authorities couldn't, or wouldn't, respond, we increased public confidence, and reporting skyrocketed in our area. So did special-crimes reporting and the successful resolution of their cases.

For once, in the history of Honduras, people had real hope they could receive justice.

But as Isaiah says: ". . . whoever shuns evil becomes a prey."

There are consequences for standing up and fighting for what is right. At first it was only various criminals who opposed our work, blaming us for their incarcerations. That was understandable. But something else began to happen. Some of the very same government authorities we were helping became angry with us.

When only 12 percent of cases go to the courts, and there is a lack of resources, it is easy to say, "We can't do anything." But when 60-70 percent of cases are resolved in the courts, something else becomes evident. Of course there will always be cases that can't be resolved. Those victims and their families must face the fact that their justice eventually will come before the throne of God.

But God says, "Let light shine out of the darkness."

When light is cast into darkness, evil deeds are exposed. This is what our ministry had been doing. Light had been cast on the corruption and negligence on the part of one judge, one or two prosecutors, many detectives, and a few police officers. We encountered cases where the same officials charged with helping victims were accepting bribes, revictimizing them, violating the law, and being negligent in their duties.

At first, when we encountered those situations, we were able to go to the chief of detectives or commanding police colonel and they made the detectives or police officers do their jobs and disciplined them for their inappropriate actions. Of course this angered them. They collaborated less and less, and we had to go to their superiors more and more.

What do you do when victims call—and they do—crying because their investigators have demanded money to move their cases? Or a woman was beaten again by her spouse because her investigator refused to take her report or gave her a citation to deliver to her aggressor to appear the next day? What do you do when a father calls pleading for help in his daughter's rape case because bribed investigators refuse to move the case to the prosecutor's office to get an arrest warrant?

"The Lord looked and was displeased that there was no justice. He saw there was no one; he was appalled that there was no one to intervene." (Isa. 59:15–16 NIV)

Fortunately, many God-fearing, wise men and women in high positions of authority within the National Police (colonels and generals) and Honduras government (presidential cabinet members) know how powerful our ministry is and, I quote, "the grand hope and help" we provide to the people. It is because of God using them that we were able to withstand the attacks of evil-hearted men and continue, although in limited ability, to serve victims.

It would be easy to throw our hands in the air, abandon the work, and leave victims powerless. It would be safer, less stressful, cheaper on the budget, and less work. But we could not abandon them.

We continued the work, reported the negligence and corruption, stood in the face of attacks and schemes launched against us. In August 2011 we filed a one-hundred-and-twenty-two-page report with the national police headquarters and the national human rights office and they both began an investigation, which of course irritated Colonel O and the investigators even more.

Salt irritates; light exposes. We are the salt and light of God.

We prayed for God to bring us a new colonel, so we could continue the work. A new colonel did arrive to take command. I met with him for more than two hours during the first week of October 2011. I told him about our ministry and the problems we had been having—how we raised special-crime closure rates, but because of the lack of collaboration, negligence, and corruption, the closure rates had fallen to 20 percent or less.

The new colonel told me he was a hard-working, honest man, who desired to bring those statistics back up, and who would ensure that officers and investigators under his command did their jobs and did them well. He said that during his first couple of weeks, he would be observing everything, investigating how things were going, and would determine what his work policies would be in Talanga. He said our ministry was very important to his country.

We hopefully waited and prayed he would see the truth and help our efforts to help victims. A week later I had another meeting with him for more than an hour. I was deeply affected by it.

He said he was trying to gain control over the disaster in Talanga and wanted to eliminate the problems. To my surprise he singled out Karina as a problem. He said she was *perjudicando* the police, specifically the DNIC agents. The Spanish word *perjudicar* means: to harm, to impair, to jeopardize. Basically, he was blaming her for the reports being filed about their corruption and negligence.

"If you wish to continue with your office here in the police station," the new colonel said, "you will need to immediately fire Karina."

I told him this was unjust because Karina had done a good job and had only acted under my authority. In addition, she hadn't filed the reports—that was my doing. He immediately dismissed my arguments, and it became clear he didn't care what they were. He didn't even want to see our reports or the evidence of what the investigators were doing.

"I don't want you speaking with anyone about what goes on here," he added. "I will settle any problems that arise. You are forbidden from reporting to *jefes* in Tegucigalpa or anyone outside of this facility. You speak only to me."

A lot of good that would do, I thought. He had surely heard about the big report I had submitted several weeks prior to his arrival. I had thought those in Tegucigalpa had answered our prayers by moving Colonel O to another post. I sensed in my spirit this man was more dangerous than his predecessor.

"It is not right for a civil nongovernmental or Christian organization to be operating inside a police department," he said, obviously irritated. "The way you are operating is completely inappropriate."

I sat on the all-too-familiar couch in front of his desk, chills running through my body, remembering the good days when meetings in this room brought justice. His rant became background sound for a few minutes as I prayed and asked the Lord what we were going to do.

"Are you listening to me?" he shouted, furious.

I held back tears as I returned my attention to the new colonel.

"The first thing you will do is fire Karina," he ordered, his voice and manner informing me this was not an option. "When you hire a new woman, you will instruct her that she is to have no contact with victims or anyone involved in their cases until the DNIC agents have completed their investigations and remitted them to the prosecutor's office. You will not be involved in their cases . . ."

His voice drifted off again as my mind went elsewhere.

He was telling me that if a bloody victim came to police headquarters for help, having to wait for hours to receive it, we were forbidden to speak to her until her case was completed. We could not help her with food or medicine or diapers or bottles, nothing. If a victim showed up and authorities refused to do their jobs, we could not advocate for her or her case.

I argued with him, but the memory of how that meeting ended is somewhere deep in the recesses of my mind. I was crushed.

I cried all the way home. I cried most of the evening, unable to eat or speak to anyone. I read and reread 2 Corinthians 4. I did not sleep that night, instead praying and wondering about what God would have us do.

The next day I had things to do in the capital and I invited Karina to go with me. During our day together, including eating lunch at a nice restaurant because I had not eaten for two days and needed a good meal for strength, we discussed the situation in Talanga.

She had known for a while the order for her to be fired was in the works, and so did I. A week before, a ranking officer in Talanga secretly informed us he overheard the DNIC plotting a way to persuade the new colonel to get rid of Karina. We discussed God's Word and how we were being persecuted for righteousness' sake. She told me what I had already had in my mind.

"Fire me," Karina said, "and move your office to the mission. Don't waste your time with them anymore."

I told her I had to pray about it.

Minutes later, a phone call changed everything. My entire world flipped upside down. Everything crumbled before me.

"You are in great danger, Gracie," the voice of a dear and trusted general said. "They are tired of you. The next time you go into the mountains with the DNIC with an arrest warrant, they have orders from higher ups to shoot you in the head. They will say there was a shootout and you were in the crossfire. We love you, so be very careful. We will be praying for you."

There it was, their final strategy. Murder. I should have known it would come to murder. It's how most battles are settled in Honduras.

Something in me changed that day. I lost my innocence: the belief that everything always came out well. I realized God didn't always stop bad things from happening. What I didn't realize then was that sometimes he allows things to happen for a greater purpose.

I read and reread 2 Corinthians 4:1–6, every line of which applied to this situation: corrupt people, blind-hearted people, and how we as Christians should respond.

"Therefore, since through God's mercy we have this ministry, we do not lose heart. Rather, we have renounced secret and shameful ways [corruption]; we do not use deception [lies], nor do we distort the Word of God. On the contrary, by setting forth the truth plainly [reporting] we commend ourselves to everyone's conscience in the sight of God [accusations against us]. And even if our gospel is veiled, it is veiled to those who are perishing [our good works veiled to those who are corrupt]. The god of this age [corruption, laziness, greed, and violence] has blinded the minds of unbelievers, so that they cannot see the light of the gospel that displays the glory of Christ, who is the image of God. For what we preach is not ourselves, but Jesus Christ as Lord, and ourselves as your servants for Jesus' sake. For God, who said, 'Let light shine out of darkness,' made his light shine in our hearts to give us the light of the knowledge of God's glory displayed in the face of Christ."

The next morning I dropped Karina at the police station and told her to put a note on the door of our office saying she was on vacation for two weeks and for them to call me if a victim needed something. Then she was to go straight home.

I went to the courthouse next to the station to meet with a judge's secretary about a case. As I walked up to the gate, I ran into the one trusted agent we knew in the DNIC. After greeting each other and hugging, he looked around as though he was making sure no one was watching us.

"I am praying for you," he whispered as he leaned closer to me. "Be very careful, Gracie, people want to hurt you."

I pretended I didn't understand and tried to wave it off. But he grabbed my arm and pulled me close.

"There are orders. Don't go anywhere in your truck with the DNIC."

He looked around again, pointed at me, touching my breastbone and said, "Don't," and walked away.

Later that day a message was conveyed through Karina to me from the new colonel that "our time was up."

I spent the night praying at home, waiting for God to intervene and instruct us to continue the fight at police headquarters in Talanga, or to back off and move the operation to the mission site in La Ermita. I was crying again when a nanny from our children's home walked into my living room.

"You have many people here in Honduras," she said. "They all love you. I hear them in the streets and in my village and on the buses talking about the powerful work God is doing through you and the hope they have. You cannot give up; they will back you."

As I prayed on my couch in the living room, the Lord reminded me of what he had said to me in May. "The office would be closed by October 31." I didn't want to receive that word. To me, it was failure. In my perspective, I had failed the Lord. I had failed the people.

The whisper came again.

"The office will be closed by October 31."

I didn't understand, but I finally heard what the Lord was telling me. It must be closed.

For now.

Just as Christ died on the cross and the hopes of the disciples vanished because they didn't know God had a plan that Christ would rise again. God had a bigger plan than what I could see or understand in the moment. It would be years before I could see the whole picture and know what I know today.

Sometimes something must die before it can grow and be great. That was what God was doing with our work. I only had to accept it and walk through it.

A few days later, the biggest corruption scandal the country had ever seen was exposed. On October 23, 2011, the son of Julieta Castellanos, the head of the university in Tegucigalpa and founder of the Observatory of Violence was murdered by four police officers. His death opened a Pandora's box exposing police cartels of organized crime and connections to gangs and drug traffickers throughout the country that would plague the nation for years to come.

On Nov. 1, 2011, I officially resigned as chief of special crimes for Talanga, Juticalpa, and Gracias. A day later we closed the office in Talanga and moved everything to our mission in La Ermita. Corrupt officials in Talanga believed, as did the Pharisees and Sadducees when Christ died, that they had won. We were out of the picture, no longer a threat to them.

The disciples only had to wait three days for their victory. We had to wait six years. But God is in the waiting. He is there moving things and influencing things we cannot see. The government and people of Honduras have struggled for years with corruption among their police.

The details of the corruption scandal blew up in April 2016. The Honduran newspaper *El Heraldo*, broke a story that top Honduran police officials were suspected of collaborating with drug traffickers, gangs, and members of organized crime. They published documents with the names and faces of the top officials suspected of criminal activities. However, all the names and faces were blurred out.

Shortly thereafter, another document, a picture of an order from Honduran national police headquarters, was released showing that an official high up in the Honduran national police forbade the newspapers and other media in Honduras from releasing names or faces of the officials implicated in their story.

I read through every article, downloaded them, and scanned them closely to see if I could recognize the faces or names, but I could not. Who were these officials? I wondered.

A week later as I read news on the internet, a *New York Times* headline caught my eye. The *New York Times* article published that day ran the same story that was in the Honduran papers, but they did not block out or blur anything. They exposed the names and faces of the top Honduran officials suspected of collaborating with drug traffickers, gangs, and members of organized crime.

The article said the officials were also allegedly ordering executions, naming two Christian friends of ours: General Julian Aristides Gonzalez Irias, head of the antinarcotics team in the police, who was murdered in December of 2009 and General Gustavo Alfredo Landaverde Hernandez, who took Aristides' position in the antinarcotics unit, and was murdered in December of 2011, just weeks after we closed our office because of threats to assassinate me.

Looking at the names and faces of those suspected to be involved, I was surprised to see that I knew almost every one of the officials whose names and faces were plastered across the *New York Times* pages. A shiver went down my spine as I realized several of these officials had received my September 2011 report on the corruption going on in Talanga. I remembered the general's warning that there was an order to kill me.

Despite knowing so many of the officials accused of wrongdoing, I also knew there were good police officers and government officials who were struggling, like we were, to combat the evil that plagues Honduras. I still keep in touch with them, I pray for them, and we still work together. A few have retired from the police force, but many continue the battle with faith that God will protect them and help them overcome the great evil and oppression that grows daily in this place.

I recently recalled something as I prayed for Honduras. Back in 2011, just before I was told about the order to assassinate me, we handled the case of a newborn infant who had been sold or given away by its mother to another couple. I think it was the last time I went with DNIC agents on a mission in my truck.

One of the police officers who had previously been assigned to my office and who had saved my life on more than one occasion, went with us when we went to recover the baby. My truck was filled with DNIC agents and police officers, maybe seven in all. We came to the house where we were told the baby was with the couple. But it was unseen from the road, hidden behind banana trees, bushes, and tropical vegetation, on a road that wove through the mountains.

The DNIC agents, as usual, told me to wait in the truck. I sat in the driver's seat and watched them run off across the pavement and disappear into the vegetation. But the officer who had previously worked with me paused in the middle of the road, looked up and down the empty mountain road, and then ran back to the truck.

Quickly, he pulled his pistol out of his holster and passed it to me through the window.

"Keep this with you," he said. "Just in case you need it."

Then he sped across the street and disappeared into the bush.

Nothing happened that day. But I often wonder if he knew about the order to kill me, and unable to warn me, had protected me in the only way he could.

The office was dead.

But death is not the end, it is only the beginning . . .

SECTION IV

REBIRTH—HE IS DOING A NEW THING

"I am Making Everything New! . . .
Write This Down,
for These Words are Trustworthy and True . . .
It is Done."
Revelation 21:5–6 (NIV)

CHAPTER THIRTEEN

ASHES STIRRING

"Forget the former things;
do not dwell on the past.
See, I am doing a new thing!"
Isaiah 43:18–19 (NIV)

Sometimes you think something is dead and gone, and then you realize it was just sleeping, waiting for the perfect moment to arise from the ashes in glory.

After many years of working alongside authorities in justice ministry with great success, we had to close the office because of a few corrupt individuals in positions of power. But we had worked side by side with many good police officers, too, individuals who loved serving the people and empowering justice for women and children suffering oppression. Many Hondurans want to make a difference.

We began this journey to justice with Colonel Roberto Alex Villanueva Meza, who set us to work during 2005. We are still on this journey to bring justice to the oppressed; to rescue them from harm, care for them and restore their lives, and to bring the love and power of God into their lives.

A great joy for me is how much the police officers delighted in working with us. Whenever we had a mission to go deep into the mountains to rescue a woman or child, issue an arrest warrant, or investigate, officers were eager to participate. They wanted to go with us.

During those years I did a lot of hands-on work alongside investigators and police, assisting with coordination of investigations and accompanying them on missions to rescue women and girls. Sometimes I would be gone for days as we did reconnaissance in remote areas where someone had been abducted, was selling babies, or prostituting girls in ranches, so we could plan a rescue or an arrest. At times we climbed through coffee fields, pushing banana leaves out of our faces as we hiked to remote locations to rescue someone.

I remember missions where the terrain was so steep that officers would grab my hands to drag me up, laughing the whole time, as others pushed me from behind. The laughter ceased when we arrived on scene. I always stayed back while officers approached the house and scouted the target. Once the area was secured, I could run in and wrap my arms around the recovered woman or children and tell them God had sent us to rescue them. I loved those days and miss them.

We taught the officers to seek God's help in their missions. If they were lined up in the courtyard in full gear, prepared for a dangerous mission, I would come out of my office, raise my hand over them and pray for their safety and success. When we went in our truck on a mission with officers, we prayed over our vehicle, team and the mission for protection, favor and success.

"*Señor, protégenos en nuestro ida y vuelta, sin novedades, sin problemas mecánicas, invisible a los que quieren hacernos daño, en el nombre de Jesús, amen.*" Lord protect us in our travel and return, without complications or incidents, without mechanical problems, invisible to those who would harm us in Jesus' name, amen.

I still pray this each time I leave the mission.

Many times we would listen to worship music on the radio or CD player as we drove through the mountains. All of us in the pickup cab singing to the Lord at the top of our lungs.

I remember one night coming back from Tegucigalpa. Officer Miguel was driving, and I was in the passenger seat. In the rear seat sat Officer Sanchez and a father and son, victims of a horrible case of rape, attempted murder, and kidnapping. The worship song *Todo Poderoso* (All Powerful) was blasting through the truck's speakers, and we were all singing, smiling, and praising God as we traveled up and around the mountains, windows open with a star-filled sky over us. It was a powerful moment I will never forget.

The officers were eager to learn how to serve the people. Discussing with them God's role in their work—how he wants us to love one another and is seeking champions to intervene in horrible situations—was pure joy. They were like sponges, absorbing everything and growing in their faith. No one had ever taught this aspect of service to them, their training being along military lines.

To watch them grow in their love for the people was amazing. To be in a village with a woman whose husband almost killed her and see officers treat her gently and pause to pray over her after she broke down in tears while giving her statement was a beautiful thing. Those days were some of the most treasured of my life.

We used to joke that we would never let Officer Sanchez pray at meals because he took so long the food would be cold by the time he finished. His testimony is amazing. Officer Sanchez had been shot seven times and taken to a section of the public hospital where, he said, "Only the dead come out with tags on their toes." His wife had been told to prepare for his burial.

Officer Sanchez had been in a cantina when "men came in and caused trouble." They chased him outside and shot him multiple times. Severely wounded, he managed to stumble down the dark, dirt road to a bridge over a tiny river.

"As I grabbed onto the railing and looked over the edge to the river below," he said, "I saw a river of blood. I prayed out to God to save me because I didn't want my children to be orphans as I had been. I told God I would give my life to him and asked him to save me. Then I passed out."

For days his family prayed in the lobby of the hospital because they were not allowed inside where Officer Sanchez was being treated. His family had bought his casket and burial plot and prepared for receiving his body when the hospital turned it over to them. One day during the family's death watch, the doctors told his wife they were bringing him out. Family members began howling in grief, certain Officer Sanchez was dead.

A gurney wheeled out with his body on it. To the shock and joy of his tearful wife, Officer Sanchez raised a hand and made a thumbs-up sign. He was alive! He was recovering. The family was stunned because the doctors had neglected to tell them he was alive. They were only told he was coming out—from the sector of the hospital where nobody emerges alive.

Officer Sanchez loves to tell his story. He will stand in the middle of a room full of missionaries recounting every detail, lifting his shirt, and twisting his body to show them the scars from the bullet holes. He revels in talking about how he died, and how God brought him back from the dead. The joy that covers his face, and the excitement in his voice as he relates his personal miracle is a treat to watch.

During the years we worked in the victims office, we counseled the police and investigators. Day by day, out in the field, sharing God's Word and love for his children. We began to see God's love reflecting from them as they cared for those who had been raped or kidnapped and in their dealing with family members of those who suffered crimes. Instead of being cold and methodical, barking questions at victims and witnesses while taking statements, they were gentle and kind. They learned patience.

The people began trusting the police, at least in cases where good officers and agents did their jobs. But in the cases where we had to fight to make investigators conduct investigations and interview witnesses, the stigma of corrupt officials and distrust of authorities became ingrained in the minds of the people. I remember afternoons sitting on the benches in front of the *guardia* with witnesses and victims, and hearing a common refrain, "If you have money and connections you can get off of anything."

Even though many officials were corrupt, many more were not. I smile as I think back on how many were excited to work with us. And of the sincerity of sergeants in remote posts calling me at two o'clock in the morning to seek advice on cases. "I want to do this right; help me," was another common refrain. They wanted to do a good job.

After we closed the offices on November 2, 2011, I often have encountered officers in the streets who would ask me when we were getting back to doing the work we had done before.

"When are you coming back," they'd ask. "We miss you. We miss the work."

Since the victims office closed, God has been moving, always going before us. There have been good days and bad days, days filled with victory and those with pain. But God always goes before us. Our followers and sponsors pray for us daily, for the strength to continue.

It has been a difficult journey. While God always opened doors for us, the weight of the task is often heavy. The challenges we face are difficult. It is hard. Everything here is hard. Nothing here is easy—except when God opens doors for his work to be done.

Difficult times helped me learn the importance of self-care. I used to just keep going, doing case after case, not taking any time off until I literally crashed and had to shut the door and go away for a day or two to rest, recover, and let the Lord fill me up.

During our first years, we were almost overcome a few times. It is hard to always live in violence. My whole life is rape, murder, sex trafficking, and kidnapping. My life is living with and in all these dark things. I have had to take crime scene photographs of decapitated women and hold children who have been raped or who had witnessed their stepfather murder their mothers.

Because it is such a difficult place to be, we must stay close to the Lord to carry on. God is full of grace. His mercy and grace are powerful when you stick close to him. I jokingly tell people that I super glue myself to Jesus because "there is no way I can do this without him."

During 2011 when the police corruption crisis hit in Honduras, we had to back off because our opponents were no longer just the friends and family of aggressors, but also included people who were supposed to be protecting us.

We closed the office, but we continued the work with authorities through our refuge and home for pregnant girls, by teaching ministries and preaching in churches about how God has called us all to stand in the gap for those who suffer. Our weekly radio show continued to reach more than half a million people. And we began preparing for God's next step.

Other challenges arose. But our battle was never against people. It was against principalities, powers, and darkness of this age. We have the advantage: darkness can never overcome the light.

Every year the Lord gives me a word or two for the year. For 2014 and 2015, the word was "endurance." Those two years were extremely difficult. I remember speaking with Pastor John Mattica, a good friend, counselor, and president of the Honduran Fellowship of Missionaries and Ministries, during the beginning of 2015 because I had not been given another word for the year 2015. He laughed when I told him.

"Maybe the Lord wants you to continue with the word you already have," he said.

I wasn't pleased because 2014 had been full of challenges and battles, and some almost wiped me out. The idea of having another year like that was overwhelming. Then 2015 proved to be even more difficult. One incident, of an American girl under our care being drugged and gang raped was so stressful, that I almost had a nervous breakdown. I wanted to pack up and leave.

But the Lord told me to rest in his embrace. I stayed home, spent time in prayer and in the Word. Taking this time to rest and be with him restored the passion I needed to continue the ministry. We must always focus on self-care throughout our work, not just when we hit the wall. I had to learn that. My husband and I began to focus on self-care, not in a selfish or lazy manner, but in a strategic and intentional way in which we planned margins in our days for rest and time with the Lord to assure we don't crash or burn out. It was one of the best decisions Lee and I have ever made.

The year 2016 arrived and God gave me a different word, two actually: confident and serious. I thought because the word endurance had been replaced, the year would be easier, but it wasn't. Throughout 2016 God demonstrated that endurance will always be needed when we serve the Lord. We need to be serious about the work we do. We must know up front that we always are going to have to "stand, and then stand therefore."

The new words he had given, confident and serious, were significant in my own personal growth. Confident meant knowing God is able and willing to do the things he has said he would do, even when I cannot see it. Having that deep knowledge of him. It also means I need to be confident that he could and would do things through me.

We are just normal people. Lee and I are just two children of God. He has called us into this work. Whoever you are, whatever your faults and failures, God can and will call you into something.

"Serious" was the other word he had given me. He wanted me to get serious about this work because the ministry was going to grow. A lot of interesting things began to happen.

During February 2015 I received a telephone call from Mercedes Bustillo, the national prosecutor for crimes against women (*Fiscalia de la Mujer Nacional*). She is an amazing lady. She told me she had a program, sort of an expanded and improved version of the one I wrote in 2005. She was working with the United Nations office to open two pilot offices to attend victims of special crimes in Francisco Morazán state. One would be in Talanga, the other in Sabanagrande, a town in a county with the same name, just south of the capital. The county, Sabanagrande, has a population of about twenty thousand people, much like Talanga.

She said when she sought people in our area to discuss the project with, everyone had told her to come speak with me. It was a Saturday morning when she called. I was excited about her project. I told her I could meet with her in her office in Tegucigalpa on Monday, but she suggested she come visit me at our ministry that same day. I was shocked she had such passion. Nobody in authority works weekends. And she was one of the nation's highest officials. This was huge.

Normally, an official in her position would travel in a government vehicle with a driver and bodyguard. But she arrived at our ministry in her personal car, alone. We had coffee and talked for about two hours. She wanted to appoint me as president of the board overseeing the new victims office to ensure things went well.

The following week her office introduced the project, known by the acronym "MAIE" (*Modelo de Atención Integral Especial*), or Model of Special and Integral Attention, at a meeting with community leaders in Talanga. To begin the work, a governing board was installed with me as president.

The program initially didn't work well in Talanga because people in that community don't like to volunteer. Every time I called board meetings, only one or two board members appeared. Finally, though, an office was opened at city hall. A woman assigned to the mayor's Office of the Woman was put in charge.

Because her office was six blocks from the police station, many victims didn't know she was there to help so the office was not nearly as effective as the one we had before. In prayer, though, God revealed this was just a first step in reviving the work we had done before and in expanding it in a much more effective way. It would not be affected by the violence and corruption we had faced before.

It was badly needed. Since our office had closed, all statistics regarding special crimes had fallen to levels even worse than before our office opened. Corruption increased, and abusers acted with near impunity. Community confidence dropped to almost zero. Hope disappeared as injustice ruled the day.

Through prayer, God showed me that closing the office was not a failure, not a negative thing. It was proof—signed, sealed, and delivered—that the work we had done was significant.

At this time God began revealing to me that we would open another office. I just wasn't sure about the how or the when, or any of the details.

Things began to unfold during 2016. One afternoon during January 2016, I heard a knock at our door. As I approached it and scanned the driveway through a window, I spotted a white pickup with tinted windows and two women standing near our gate. They introduced themselves as being with Compassion International, a Colorado-based, child-advocacy ministry. They wanted to speak with us.

Lee and I served them coffee in our family room. It's a moment that remains crystal clear in my memory. Late afternoon sun fell into the indoor patio, the children were playing in the yard, and there was an overall element of peace and anticipation.

One of the women explained they were working on a project with their CDI program (*Centro Desarrollo Integral*) or Center for Integral Development, a program for children at risk. She said Compassion International had realized that violence against women and children was an issue the organization needed to become involved in and address within the communities it served. Conferences were scheduled throughout Honduras with twenty to forty church pastors and CDI program directors. She said someone was needed to instruct conference attendees about Honduras law and procedures regarding violence against women and children.

They wanted me to speak at a conference in the Valley of Angels, with a group of pastors and CDI leaders from Tegucigalpa and a few surrounding villages in attendance. She said they had been looking everywhere for someone who knew the subject and were invariably told to talk to me.

After the Valley of Angels conference, they wanted me to go to each church and each CDI program to deliver the same message, a presentation known as "Called to Rescue—Stand in the Gap." It is the same presentation I have made to leaders, students, and authorities since our ministry began. About twenty-five events planned in collaboration with Compassion International came out of this one meeting.

What they didn't know is the "Called to Rescue" presentation isn't limited to just laws and procedures in special-victim cases. It is saturated with God's heart for justice.

I remember well the day I presented "Called to Rescue" in the Valley of Angels. I was given about ninety minutes for the lecture. The tables were organized in a "U" shape. This gave me not only space at the end, but also room to come face-to-face with attendees as I spoke. I do not like to stand behind a podium or be attached to a microphone and wire when I speak. I like to move around and sometimes get into people's faces.

That day the Holy Spirit moved with great power during my presentation. They loved it, received it, and clearly understood God's call to stand in the gap and rescue those who are oppressed.

During a coffee break after my presentation, I remember sitting alone at the table. The pastors all grouped together in one area talking with each other, the CDI directors were doing the same in another area. The Compassion staff had left the room.

I went outside to take a walk under the coconut trees and palms, among the gardens, looking for a restroom when I noticed the Compassion staff huddled on the grass in what appeared to be an intense discussion. A couple looked over at me as I passed. I waved and continued my search for a bathroom.

Later when I returned to my seat at the table, ready to hear the next presentation, three of the Compassion leaders walked over and put a piece of paper on the table in front of me. On it was the list and schedule of the remaining conferences in Honduras. They wanted me to commit to speak at all of the remaining conferences and the follow-up meetings for churches and CDI programs.

I was speechless.

They were standing around me as the next presenter began teaching, whispering what they wanted me to do. The energy and excitement in their faces and voices overwhelmed me. I told them we had only contracted this one event and then the follow-up meetings.

"We have never heard a presentation of the law like this, integrating the Word of God, as you have done," the group's leader said, her body trembling with excitement, her face animated.

"That was the most dynamic and powerful presentation we have ever seen on the laws! And God's Word was in all of it; it was engaging and interesting. Usually a lawyer does it for us and it is boring and lifeless. But this . . ." she trailed off. "We were all profoundly affected."

They said they had all gone outside after my presentation was finished to discuss it, and all had agreed they desired for me to make the same presentation at all their conferences.

I could have become swell-headed and thought myself grand with all the wonderful things they were saying. But the truth be told, I knew that it was God, not me, who had put it all together. He gave me the words and the way to present it. I was stunned by their request as I pondered the responsibility of agreeing to give so many presentations, somewhere between seventy and a hundred.

I looked again at the list of conferences and where they were being held, then I looked back up at them.

"I will pray about it," I said.

I confess, I never listened to the presentation occurring in front of me. I stared at the list and prayed.

"Lord, what do you want me to do?"

So many events and travel were involved. When the conference broke for lunch, I called the director over and told her that after praying, the Lord showed me that I could do all of the conferences except one, which was too far away. In the end I had agreed to about seventy events. Throughout 2016 and 2017, we were able to realize about thirty of those events and my participation continues to this day.

At the end of April 2016, I went to the United States to be with my daughter who was giving birth to my second grandchild. While with her, I was contacted by Lenni Benson, who is a professor of law at New York Law School and founder and senior advisor at Safe Passage Project. She asked me to speak at a Continuing Legal Education, or CLE, conference on immigration during the first week of June. I had been a country condition expert on violence against women and children and gang violence in Honduras since 2008, testifying in about forty asylum cases in U.S. Immigration Court.

I had spoken the previous year at a CLE unaccompanied minor conference at Charles Widger School of Law at Villanova University at the request of Michele Pistone, head of the legal clinic there. Michele had spoken with Lenni about doing another conference and I was asked, among others, to speak.

To speak at New York Law School, I had to extend my time in the United States by about ten days. After making flight changes, my Twitter feed was filled with notices that the Justice Conference in Chicago was scheduled for a couple days before the New York event. I had always wanted to go to the annual Justice Conference, but never could for lack of money and time. I found myself just ninety minutes from Chicago where the Justice Conference was being held.

I was there and had time, but I still had another problem: money. Our ministry didn't have enough money to pay for my airfare and hotel to the New York event. I was personally paying for it. Lee and I received only a small salary ($450 a month each) because we prefer the money go into programs. I didn't have the money to pay for a bus to Chicago, Uber transport, hotel, food, and Justice Conference fees.

However, I felt deep within me that the Lord had orchestrated this for me to attend the conference. If I hadn't been asked to speak in New York and changed my flight, I would not have been in the United States—or the Chicago area—during the dates of the Justice Conference. What to do? I prayed.

"Just ask," the Lord whispered.

Before going to bed that night, I posted in our Facebook group page the need and desire to attend the conference. The next morning as I read correspondence, I found an email from one of our sponsors saying she was sending $1,000 to cover both conferences' expenses. I stared at the email, tears streaming down my face.

I registered for the Justice Conference and chose the refugee preconference workshop because I was speaking three days later about immigration in New York. I figured I might learn something useful for my presentation there. However, the night before I left for Chicago, I received a telephone call from the conference stating that the refugee preconference workshop had been canceled. The only other options I had were one on sex trafficking and another called Gospel Justice. I started to tell her I wanted the sex trafficking workshop, but something inside me made me hesitate. I looked at the Gospel Justice description again.

"Sign me up for the Gospel Justice workshop," I said.

Little did I know that God was going to blow open his plans for our ministry with that one small decision. At the preconference workshop I met Bruce Strom, founder of Administer Justice and president, founder of the Gospel Justice Initiative and author of *Gospel Justice*[3], which provides pro bono legal services and is building Gospel Justice teams throughout the United States. The workshop was amazing, and I had the opportunity to speak with Bruce, his wife, Helen, Brent Amato, and others in the field of gospel justice ministry.

I learned a great deal that day and spent the rest of the Justice Conference with Bruce and his wife, Helen, whom I adore. After returning to Honduras, we began communicating and entered into a partnership. The victims office we thought God wanted us to open was just a small portion of the vision unfolding before our eyes. We entered into a partnership with Bruce and Gospel Justice Initiative to open a Gospel Justice Center in Honduras. It would be the first Gospel Justice center outside the United States and the first in Latin America.

---

3   Bruce Strom, *Gospel Justice* (Chicago: Moody Publishers 2013).

When I look back on things and think about the tapestry the Lord weaves in our lives, I can't help but notice the little events that happen one after another along the way. Had any one of them been absent, none of this would have come to pass. It was a domino effect. One tile falls, then another and another until we find ourselves doing amazing things that are bigger and better than anything we could have dreamed on our own.

If my daughter hadn't been having a baby, I would not have been in the Chicago area. If I hadn't been asked to speak in New York, I would not have extended my trip and been able to go to the Justice Conference. If the sponsor had not sent the money, I would not have been able to go to Chicago. If the refugee preconference workshop had not been canceled, I would not have met Bruce Strom, and so it goes.

Then there was Beth Lyons, head of the clinic at Villanova Law School, who did a search on violence and Honduras in 2008 looking for someone to help her with an asylum case and my name popped up. Through her, I met Michele Pistone. If that had not happened, and we hadn't worked together on many asylum cases, I would not have been asked to speak at Villanova in 2015, which also would have prevented me from speaking at New York Law School in 2016.

Many things in our lives occur as part of the tapestry God weaves in our lives. Most of them we never notice. Some we call coincidence or luck. But, good or difficult, I believe it is all part of God's plan.

The ashes of the work we thought had died in 2011 were beginning to stir. God was moving on something bigger than we had previously accomplished. Something far grander than we could have imagined. We were about to come face-to-face with the next step of our destiny.

"Brothers and sisters, I do not consider myself yet to have taken hold of it. But one thing I do: Forgetting what is behind and straining toward what is ahead, I press on toward the goal to win the prize for which God has called me heavenward in Christ Jesus." (Phil. 3:13–14 NIV)

CHAPTER FOURTEEN

DEFINING MOMENTS

"He changes times and seasons; he deposes kings and raises up others. He gives wisdom to the wise and knowledge to the discerning. He reveals deep and hidden things; he knows what lies in darkness, and light dwells within him."
Daniel 2:21–22 (NIV)

Throughout our lives there are defining moments, which could pass by unnoticed if we are not paying attention to what God is doing. If we do notice them, we might consider them to be luck or chance instead of predestined moments God puts in place to lead us to our destiny.

During 2015 through 2017, God orchestrated many defining moments, leading us on the path he was creating for us to become leaders in justice ministry, not only in Honduras, but throughout the United States and Central and South America.

After the victims offices in Talanga, Juticalpa, and Gracias were closed, we continued working with area authorities through our refuge and girls home and participating in conferences and teaching events throughout the country. We believed God would bring us to a point where we again would have an office to serve victims during crises.

The 2011 office closings only served to emphasize the real need for them. Violence against women and children was becoming more prominent around the nation. Crimes against women increased 267 percent, and more than five thousand women were murdered between 2005 and 2016. The United Nations reported a 94-96 percent impunity rate in all cases of violence against women and children in Honduras. Corruption was rampant.

We saw many defining moments, signals from God that he was beginning this part of the work again. Talanga had a new office to attend victims of violence and and we were put in charge of the committee to oversee it, and a partnership was launched with Gospel Justice Initiative to bring their justice center program to Honduras. The dominoes were falling.

Because of many challenges and attacks on us and the ministry, I kept asking the Lord, "Why am I living in this cycle where I do advocacy, serve, stand up for something, and then face attacks?" This has been a pattern in my life. I stand up for God and do something, then the attacks come through people and circumstances. I wondered what was wrong with me.

At a missionary retreat in Honduras during February 2015, a pastor discussed identity in Christ.

"Can you identify one Scripture that defines who God created you to be?" he asked.

I knew instantly. For me it was Isaiah 59:14–16 (NIV), specifically verse 16.

"So justice is driven back, and righteousness stands at a distance; truth has stumbled in the streets, honesty cannot enter. Truth is nowhere to be found, and whoever shuns evil becomes a prey. The Lord looked and was displeased that there was no justice. He saw that there was no one, he was appalled that there was no one to intervene."

This is what my life is all about: shunning evil, taking a stand and becoming a target. This is my Scripture, my purpose, my identity, my destiny—to be one who intervenes. This is what justice ministry is about. It is in my blood; it is who I am. For me, not standing up and helping someone is like not breathing.

I never understood why I was so compelled to stand up when I saw suffering. In the Spanish version of this Scripture it uses the word "*disgustado*." God was disgusted to see there was no one to intervene. That word impacts me: disgusted. All I can think of is our all-powerful Father looking down upon this earth, disgusted to see the violence against his children, disgusted to see that there is no one to intervene. He sees all this injustice, all this oppression, and he is disgusted.

A victim once asked me why it took twenty years for God to rescue her from the child abuse and spousal abuse she suffered. I told her I believe there are two reasons why victims of violence are not rescued. One is that sometimes victims are not ready to be rescued. They keep returning to their aggressors. No rescue with permanent restoration is possible until they desire to change their lives.

The other reason is there is no one there to rescue them. Those who God has called to do the rescuing are disobedient and/or absent. These are situations where if Jesus doesn't show up, there is no hope. Someone remains trapped in sex trafficking, domestic violence, or sexual abuse because no one shows up to rescue them.

I also believe oppression continues because people don't stand up against it.

I want to drive this point home. When Christians run into situations, they generally respond saying they will pray for the person, but they do nothing to help them. They say it isn't their problem or they shouldn't get involved. But God is calling us to act. The Bible says faith without action is dead.

All of this leads to action, to hope. If you are in a dark room and you light a candle, the darkness recedes. Can you imagine if everyone united in doing something—anything? It doesn't have to be justice ministry; it could be something else.

Our work cannot be done without prayers, without people coming to help us, and without financial support. We must buy food for the children, we have medical bills for girls having babies, and victims who come to us covered in blood and bruises.

We must pay salaries for a person to run the refuge and home, for a nurse to care for our clients, for nannies to care for the children, for a woman to cook the food, a person to receive cases, a person to advocate for victims. These jobs at our ministry provide income and support for single mothers and their families in a country with a 70 percent poverty rate. These women not only have a job to support their families, but the job is also an opportunity for them to serve the Lord and learn to serve their neighbors. They are participating in God's justice.

How many of God's children are called to do something yet do nothing? All of us are called to do something. Our salvation is only the first step in our life's journey with him.

"Before I formed you in the womb I knew you, before you were born I set you apart; I appointed you as a prophet to the nations." (Jer. 1:5 NIV)

God has chosen each one of us for a purpose. We all have a destiny he planned before our conception. But many Christians live passively, ignoring his call on their lives. And others don't believe that God would call them. But he specifically says he has chosen us "before" he formed us in the womb.

"Alas, Sovereign Lord," I said, "I do not know how to speak, I am too young." But the Lord said to me, "Do not say, 'I am too young.' You must go to everyone I send you to and say whatever I command you. Do not be afraid of them, for I am with you and will rescue you, declares the Lord." (Jer. 1:6–8 NIV)

Many of us, including myself, feel unworthy or unqualified to be called by God. We don't step forward because we don't feel worthy. But God has called each of us to something. I constantly ask myself how it is possible someone like me could be doing this work? But I am compelled to do it. And each time I do, there is backlash by those who oppress others.

With all the attacks and challenges we were facing, I had many doubts about who I was and why God always put me into situations where I had to stand up and then suffer for it.

As I prayed and asked God one night in early 2016 why he chose me for this task, he told me to go to Amazon.com and type in "stand in the gap." I had this image of standing in the gap for victims, thinking about how God had called me to be a person who intervenes.

I went online to Amazon.com and typed in "stand in the gap," and a book by Pastor Wilfredo de Jesus, from the Chicago area called, *In the Gap: What Happens When God's People Stand Strong*[4], popped up. I bought the Kindle version and read half the book that night. Since then I have read it four times. I finally realized the why behind my questions.

In his book, Pastor Choco, a name he is known by, talks about Ezekiel 22:30 where God was speaking to Ezekiel about people living in corruption and violence, where injustice reigned and there was nobody to stand in the gap to defend his children.

"The people of the land practice extortion and commit robbery; they oppress the poor and needy and mistreat the foreigner, denying them justice. I looked for a man among them who would build up the wall and stand before me in the gap on behalf of the land so I would not have to destroy it, but I found none." (Ezek. 22:29–30 NIV)

God is looking for people to stand in the gap, and that is what he has us doing in Honduras—and soon to be doing throughout all of Latin America.

---

4   Wilfredo de Jesus, *In the Gap: What Happens When God's People Stand Strong* (Springfield, Missouri: Influence Resources 2014).

This work, right down to the very first day when the colonel showed up at our mission and said, "We need you to stand in the gap." He didn't use those exact words, but that was what he meant. We were to be that bridge between the people and the police.

Since that day we have been standing in the gap for thousands of people who have suffered violence. In the years we had the victims offices at the police station and I was chief of special crimes, we handled more than six thousand cases. Those were the actual police reports that were filed. Each case represented a minimum of one victim, but some had as many as eight.

Those six thousand or so cases did not include all the telephone calls for counsel and help, nor the people who showed up at our door, nor those who stopped me in the streets. It also doesn't include those who heard our programs on the radio and were helped, nor the sixty thousand or so people who were present in events I taught and preached throughout the country.

We are teaching those who suffer that there is help; there is a way out of their troubles. We are training pastors, leaders, and authorities—thousands of them—to stand in the gap and help those who suffer oppression. We are teaching police officers how to respond to those who seek help and teaching the prosecutors and investigators how to best treat the victims they are supposed to serve. We are calling the corrupt to accountability.

Then there are the pastors, leaders, and ministries we are teaching to recognize victims in their midst and what they need to do to help them, and what they are commanded by God to do. We are walking with them through the rescue, care, restoration, and justice processes. We are teaching them to be people who change nations and circumstances around them.

We are teaching the people that when a man becomes violent with his wife there are consequences. When a man abuses a child, there will be consequences. Victims know there is someone out there with arms opened wide, ready to help them out of their distress. God himself is sending rescue, help and, restoration. God himself is providing justice.

I asked the Lord, "Why am I like this?" And he sent me to Pastor Choco via Amazon.com, whose book helped me understand what was "wrong with me." What was "wrong" with me is that God put this heart of Christ in me. He put a desire that compels me to stand in the gap and stand up and do something.

"Christ's love compels us . . ." (2 Cor. 5:14 NIV)

Darkness can only overcome light when we choose to surrender. The light within us comes from God and we choose to surrender or to shine. It is a choice we all make. When we surrender or become indifferent to the suffering around us, our light dims—or goes out. But if we choose to shine and stand against the darkness of this world, our single light overcomes the darkness just by being lit.

His love in us compels us to shine our light in dark places. One with a true heart for Christ lives a life that reflects him and his love.

I learned there was nothing wrong with me at all. Through the attacks and endurance, God had been teaching me to stand firm in the storms of life. We must endure. We cannot give up because if we give up, then those who are suffering oppression remain in darkness.

"So justice is driven back, and righteousness stands at a distance; truth has stumbled in the streets, honesty cannot enter. Truth is nowhere to be found, and whoever shuns evil becomes a prey. The Lord looked and was displeased that there was no justice. He saw that there was no one, he was appalled (disgusted) that there was no one to intervene." (Isa. 59:14–16 NIV)

Will you be one who intervenes? Or will you be someone who says, "Oh, that is a big problem, I can't do anything."

God can do anything with anyone. God can and will use you. He is using us to do amazing things. He is opening the doors for ministry that are beyond what we can possibly comprehend, beyond what we think we are qualified to do. He is equipping and enabling us, just as he will equip and enable you.

Everything I suffered in my life, all of the bad decisions, the blessings, the different jobs I held, my studies at university, and all the things I have ever done in my entire life—specialized foster care, advocating for women and children, counseling and helping victims of violence, having been a victim of domestic violence, of rape and assault, of emotional and psychological abuse—all of these things God is using.

The years I worked as a journalist, years writing Christian television shows, web work, poetry writing, investigative work, the degree I received from the University of North Alabama in general studies with focuses in English, communications, business financial management and justice studies—all of these things I have done in my life culminate for this time . . . for this moment . . . for this work.

God did not send someone to rape me when I was twenty-one years old and leave me pregnant, ashamed, and alone. But he knew it was going to happen and he is using it for me to be able to understand the minds and the hearts of women who have been raped and left pregnant, for women whose husbands abuse them, for those who suffer psychological torture.

The years I suffered without enough money to pay bills and buy food helped me to understand single women who are struggling to make ends meet. I know what it is like to have a man hit me and insult me, to throw me against the wall, and try to kill me. By understanding their hearts and minds, God can use me to restore their lives.

"We know that in all things God works for the good of those who love him, who have been called according to his purpose. For those God foreknew he also predestined to be conformed to the image of his Son, that he might be the firstborn among many brothers and sisters. And those he predestined, he also called; those he called, he also justified; those he justified, he also glorified." (Rom. 8:28–30 NIV)

While God did not cause these things to happen to me, he predestined I would walk this path, this journey with him to rescue others. There was no one there to rescue me. I was alone, but then I was not alone. I had Christ Jesus with me every step.

Christ also suffered injustice. Those he loved betrayed him. He was unjustly arrested and mocked and spit on. He was beaten for reasons of jealousy, contempt, hatred, and fear. He was put on trial, unjustly accused, unjustly convicted, and unjustly murdered.

He knows our suffering. He is with us through our suffering. He brings us rescue and then uses us to help others in the midst of their oppression.

During those two years—2016 and 2017—as the dominoes started to fall, the things that began to happen, were preparation for us to begin the work again in an effective way that touches thousands of lives and brings hope and rescue in not only Honduras but also in other countries too.

We reopened the victims office in Talanga, F.M., Honduras, with the collaboration of Gospel Justice Initiative on Sept. 13, 2018. The first day of operations we rescued a seventeen-year-old girl who had been raped and helped her navigate the brutal justice system. She spent a week with us in our refuge/shelter receiving love and care until her rapist went to jail and she could safely be returned to her family.

The second day we rescued a woman and her two babies from an abusive man and brought her to our refuge where God is restoring her life. The fourth day, a thirteen-year-old was sexually abused by her father. He was in the jailcell and she, her mother, and baby sister were in our refuge until trial a few days later when he was condemned and sent to prison. God is working healing and restoration in her case.

We find ourselves, through these "accidental" introductions and meetings reopening the victims office, beginning the building and opening the first Gospel Justice Center in all of Latin America (the foundation was finished Aug 15, 2018), and teaching missionaries, churches, leaders, and other NGOs the justice model and how to recognize victims in their midst—and what to do when they do find them.

During these next months and years, in collaboration with other ministries, we will build a Latin American Justice Coalition, linking all ministries and institutions who serve victims of crimes together with God, for justice, restoration, and redemption.

The power of God is moving in this place, he is cleansing, healing, and ministering his grace.

While listening to a man give his testimony at a Celebrate Recovery meeting I served food at, I heard him say, "We have to choose if we will make our pain and suffering our master, or our servant."

Powerful words. Our Father flips everything upside down. He uses the weak to confound the wise. He uses the broken to change nations. Those who believe they are worthless and have nothing to give are the very ones he will choose to use.

We endured almost seven years with our victims office closed. But today it is open again, serving those who find themselves lost in darkness.

We must stand, shine, and endure. We cannot surrender. If we do and our light goes out, then those who suffer oppression remain in the darkness.

CHAPTER FIFTEEN

LOVE ME

"holy and dearly loved"
Colossians 3:12

I believe it is time I came clean and told you the truth. My name is not Gracie, but it *is* Gracie. I was born Robin Claire Travis. It took about thirty years for the Lord to transform me into Gracie, and now most people don't even know that Robin existed. Part of me prefers it that way because every time I hear the name Gracie, I am reminded of all God has done for me.

Just as Abram became Abraham, Sarai became Sarah, Saul became Paul, Simon became Peter, and many others received new identities when God put his fingerprint on their lives, Robin became Gracie. It is hard for me to remember exactly when it happened, but I believe it was around 1996. But first, I believe I owe it to you to explain who Robin was before she disappeared—or rather before she was transformed and redeemed.

Robin was the kind of woman who was broken in so many ways that it seemed impossible for anyone or anything to be able to fix her. The wounds and scars in her life were so profound, only complete annihilation could rectify things. At least she thought so. But God delights in creating something beautiful out of brokenness.

I believe that is why I love butterflies. They go into a death phase of hibernation where a complete transformation takes place, emerging from their tomb as a new and beautiful creature. I don't have to wonder about what goes on inside that cocoon because I spent a few years in there myself before the Gracie you now see emerged.

While I lived a generally normal and happy childhood, there were certain events that deeply impacted me. Those events, combined with growing up in an atmosphere with an undercurrent of having to always strive to be approved, always falling short, never feeling like I was good enough—and being told many times I was not—took me down a path during my early adulthood years of self-destruction and low self-esteem.

I did not grow up in a Christian family. It wasn't until I was in elementary school when my mother took me to church. I only have a few memories of occasional visits to a Methodist church and being in Sunday school during that period of my life. Even there I failed because the other children knew the Bible stories I didn't, and I felt like the proverbial fish out of water when they held Bible quizzes and everyone but me knew the answers.

During adolescence, when we moved to the town where my mother grew up, church and youth group were more of a social club than a place where my faith and my knowledge of who God was grew. I had a deep love for God even though I didn't know anything about him. I desired his approval and love, but no one had ever spoken of or shared the plan of salvation with me while I was growing up. I never heard it in the Methodist church I grew up in outside of Boston. But even then he was reaching out to me and calling me into his family.

My father was in the Navy when he married my mother in the suburbs of Boston during 1963. I was only ten weeks old when they moved to the suburbs of San Francisco to be near his family, and I have few memories of that time before we moved back to the Boston area when I was five. I was three when my sister came home from the hospital, and I recall watching my mother change her diaper. I remember the first time they let me hold her and how excited I was to be a big sister.

The only other memories I can clearly recall were visiting my grandparents and Papa Eddie cooking his spaghetti sauce, the first time I saw snow when it fell in San Francisco from a freak storm, a tree falling in front of our house from another storm that spawned a tornado, and the day I was having lunch with my father and sister, eating corn chowder when an earthquake hit. I can still see my mother's china cups swinging on their hooks and hear my baby sister crying while we huddled in a doorway waiting for the shaking to stop.

But there is one more prominent memory of that time when I was four or five years old. We were visiting my paternal grandparents, and everyone was on the patio. I had been encouraged to go off and play and was excited to find some neighborhood children. I don't recall what we were playing, but I do have pieces of a memory when they grabbed me, pulled down my pants, and looked at and touched my private parts. I was crying, kicking and screaming, but no one came to help me. It wasn't long after that we moved back to the Boston area.

These days many people live in closed houses with air conditioning and children don't play outside much during the summer. But my elementary days were filled with running through the neighborhood, playing outside until dark, making forts in the woods, playing hide and seek, and other games.

A boy a year older than me lived next door. He had an older sister, and there were a few other houses on our street with children. But when the neighborhood children all gathered together to play, I was the subject of bullying.

I was a chubby child and not as physically adept as the others. I was also intelligent and loved books. They would tease me for the name Robin and run around shouting and singing "Batman!" or they would chant, "Robin

D-U-M-B Travis!" It was devastating. I just wanted to be liked and be a part of the games.

I was also the target of other bullies when I entered first grade. Because both of my parents worked, after class I went to a babysitter's house down the street from my elementary school. The babysitter's son frequently beat me up. During winter I remember being forced to sit on the ground as chunks of snow and ice from the snowplow piles were broken over my head. Those were not fond days for me.

Then there was the time a babysitter brought her boyfriend to our house and made a game of filming my baby sister's private parts with our father's movie camera.

Just as I was entering middle school, the boy next door wanted to change our Barbie and Ken games. We used to play Barbies—he had a Ken doll—and it was normal childhood stuff until he started making Barbie and Ken go to bed together and wanted to act it out in real life.

Some might dismiss these incidents as innocent childhood play, but they weren't for me. They brought shame into my life and feelings of unworthiness.

These incidents aside, there were also many wonderful childhood memories, such as going to my maternal grandmother's cottage on a lake in New Hampshire for weekends and summer vacation, and later camping in the mountains of Maine and New Hampshire. Those are joyous memories, times we were free to play and swim and be together with family.

While life appeared normal throughout my childhood—especially to outsiders—there was an undercurrent throughout that destabilized my life and sense of identity. I wasn't consciously aware of it until many years later. These are the things families keep hidden in the closet. No one wants to admit it was there, but it was, and freedom only comes when we shed light on things the enemy wants to keep hidden.

The Bible says there is power of life and death in the tongue. God spoke the world into existence, and I believe the things we say have an acute effect on our lives, development, and how we relate to others. Throughout my life there was an undercurrent of emotional abuse—such as using approval and disapproval to control people, manipulation, and using insults disguised as jokes. As an adult, I have learned that the words we use have a profound effect in building up people or destroying them.

As far back as I can remember, I was always striving to gain my father's approval. Report cards were met with cash rewards based on the grades we received and disapproval if we didn't do well enough. I distinctly remember my first "C" grade, and even though I had tried as hard as I could, it didn't matter. My father's rebuke that I had failed in his eyes profoundly hurt. But it wasn't just grades. I remember being instructed about how I spoke, that I wasn't allowed to have the Boston accent and needed to pronounce my words in a manner that didn't sound "uneducated."

There was always a struggle thrown at me and my sister as to who was the favorite, who was loved the most, who had the approval—and who didn't. Looking back on those times, I believed it was only me and my sister who struggled, but my mother also struggled. During my junior year I noticed something began happening to her.

I was young when the dinosaur nightmares began. I began dreaming about a dinosaur tearing through our neighborhood trying to devour my family. In the morning I sat on the cover of the toilet while my father shaved and told him about the dream. He dismissed it. But, to me, something was wrong. Something my child's brain was registering. I had that dream every night for a long period of time.

It was also during this time that my parents began to argue. I remember sitting with my sister on her bed talking about divorce and with whom we would choose to live. During that time, dinosaurs haunted my dreams every night and then suddenly they stopped. I later learned that my parents had discussed divorce but had decided to stay together.

The dinosaur dreams returned my junior year when my mother began to sink into a profound depression and the arguments returned. Every night my mother reclined on the couch and disappeared into a book. My father was sometimes present, sometimes not, and many times I heard raised voices when they were both in the house.

One day stands out in memory more than the others. I sat at the top of the basement stairs listening to my father on the telephone in the basement talking with his mother. The content remains clear in my mind almost forty years later. I heard him telling his mother that my mother was mentally ill, and he was going to have a friend of his commit her to a mental institution.

Panic describes how I felt in that moment, an all-encompassing panic and knowledge that my life was about to change drastically. And it did.

During the summer of my junior year, my mother moved out of our house into her mother's house on the other side of town. My family's brokenness no longer simmered under the surface, hidden from sight where we could pretend there was nothing wrong, all the while desperately trying to believe everything would be all right. This was when mental illness began to make its presence known in my sister's life with occasional bouts of violence and anger, as well as threats of suicide.

My reaction to our broken family was to dull it in teenage drinking parties and boys. Mother moved back into our home and my father moved out. I always knew when he had come back to the house by the status of my mother's emotional condition. One night is indelibly marked by a broken statue on the floor and divorce became a reality. With my father gone, my desire for acceptance grew stronger. It became an all-encompassing need.

It was as though his absence forever marked me as rejected.

While I was struggling in my own way, seeking love and acceptance in boys and dulling the pain with alcohol, I was unable to see the effects on my sister as she began to tumble into a dark world filled with depression and voices. My father had found a woman and moved in with her and her two daughters. I felt betrayed and am sure my sister did too. He had a new family and didn't want us—at least that is how it felt at the time.

Looking back on it now I understand we were all broken people looking for love and acceptance—even my father and his new family unit. They also emerged from a traumatic divorce. But, being a child in a divorce, I couldn't see it then.

My father remarried, and this woman became my stepmother. At the time, I rejected her and was angry with her for taking my father. I also rejected her daughters and didn't want anything to do with them; however, I still wanted and needed my father's love and acceptance. Those were rough times for all of us and every hateful word, misunderstood action, and error made by all parties involved became foundation stones for years of difficulties.

My mother also remarried a short time after I moved out to live at college during my freshman year. It was all I could do to get out of the situation and put as much distance as I could from the brokenness. I could pretend my life was great while partying with friends, skipping classes, and pretending everything was good. I realize now that my leaving left my baby sister alone and unprotected, trying to navigate everything on her own. I had abandoned her and my mother for my own selfish needs and desires.

My first stepfather was a violent man. His violence and manipulation not only affected my mother, but it also turned its attention on my little sister. She not only suffered secondhand violence by witnessing what he did to my mother, she also was one of his victims.

Trying to bond with my fifteen-year-old sister, I invited her to spend the weekend with me at my apartment in Boston. That Friday night I took her out to the bar I frequented with the brothers from the fraternity with whom I partied away most of my freshman year. It was a mistake that haunts me to this day. I desired to be the cool big sister, let her know I loved her and wanted to have some fun with her amid the chaos our lives had become.

She became drunk, very drunk, and called herself an ambulance. The night is a blur to me of red lights, my sister being taken away on a stretcher and then standing in the emergency room feeling helpless and terrified she would die. I don't even remember how I made it to the hospital.

Regret and self-condemnation fell on me as rain falls from the skies during a downpour. I was in the middle of a hurricane of emotions with my world ferociously twirling out of control around me. The moment I saw my father and his wife approach, I felt a mixture of relief that someone was there to help and condemnation for the bad thing I had done.

This incident confirmed everything in my life that said I was worthless and stupid.

"Beat me, hit me!" I screamed as I ran toward them in a drunken haze.

I screamed it over and over as the guilt, shame, and fear for my sister's life washed over me. I needed them to do it, though they never had hit me before, because I was worthless and deserved it. I believed in that instant that the only way I could come out of this was if I was punished severely for my lack in judgement. Unfortunately my screams brought social services into their lives and suspicions by authorities of child abuse.

My sister survived the alcohol, but my relationship with my father and his wife took a turn for the worse and has never recovered. From that point forward, the underlying current of always having to strive for acceptance became permanent disappointment, embarrassment, and rejection—at least from my perspective. I believed I was unworthy, unloved, and unaccepted, and that began to play out in most of the decisions I made in my life for years to come.

I do not want to go through all of the details of what happened during those years and since, nor do I believe I need to do so. Even now there is constant animosity, rejection, and lists of things I have done wrong during almost forty years.

Through the years I have wanted three things: forgiveness, love, and acceptance. I have learned to forgive and deeply desire a relationship with them both but must face the fact it might never come to pass. I truly believe they are broken too, and I pray every day for their healing and forgiveness, hoping that one day things would change. For all this pain, hatred, and unforgiveness to be behind us is a dream I still hold today. Each day I choose to love them.

During recent years I have learned that my brokenness and identity had their roots in the constant lack of acceptance and unforgiveness. I was bad, not accepted, not forgivable, not approved, and not worthy of their love.

Relationship with my sister has been difficult, but more so because of the things she has suffered and the mental illness that took control of her life during her late teen years. I love her deeply but am at a loss on how to relate to her because her pain and illness can be ugly and violent. I sometimes ask the Lord why he allowed her to be the one who became sick.

"Why couldn't it have been me?" I'd ask him, thinking maybe I would have been stronger to fight off the voices, suicide attempts, and darkness that consumed her.

As I entered my twenties, there was a presence of "not good enough" hiding below the surface. When I was eighteen, I met a young man who had been two years ahead of me in school and had been a hockey star. He asked me to go to a party with him. I was so excited; he liked me and noticed me!

Later that evening he picked me up, but he didn't take me to a party. He took me to a dirt road, pulled over, offered me a joint, grabbed me by the hair at the back of my head, and forced me to give him oral sex. Shame covered me when he dropped me off in my driveway an hour later. How could I tell anyone? It was my fault for believing he would take me to a party. No one would believe me. I kept that hidden deep within my heart with many other failures and bad decisions. Besides, it was another confirmation I was worthless.

My life became a series of boyfriends as I sought the love and acceptance I so desperately needed. Some I slept with, some I did not. Sex was always a difficult issue for me because of the shame I had felt from multiple incidents of touching, abuse, and the sexual attack when I was eighteen.

When I was twenty-one, I met a man through a mutual friend. He took me out on dates that seemed more like business opportunities for him than actual dates. He owned a screen-printing business, and during our first two dates left me at the bar while he met with bands to discuss business.

Each of those two nights he took me home offering only a kiss and the promise of another date. During the second date he told me he was going on vacation in Mexico and would call me when he returned. I told him I had always been fascinated with Mayan culture, and he said he would be touring the ruins in Mexico and would take pictures and show them to me when he returned.

After his trip to Mexico, he took me to an Italian restaurant. I remember I had ordered lasagna that night. Being a weekend, there was a long wait to be seated. The restaurant didn't serve alcohol, we could buy it and bring it in. He went to a liquor store to buy a bottle of wine he wanted to have with our dinner.

I remember sitting in the tight hallway filled with people, drinking the wine from a red, plastic cup filled with ice while we waited. During dinner he showed me pictures and talked about his trip to Mexico. I looked through the photos but was confused because there were no pictures of the Mayan ruins. He assured me he went there, shared a tale of climbing the steps, and seeing the view from the top. But there were no pictures. Everything else he had done was present, but not the one thing I had wanted to see.

"I must have left them in my apartment," he said. "We can swing by there before I take you home."

I agreed. He lived on the third floor of a three-family, triple-decker house. The apartment décor and disaster within demonstrated it was definitely occupied by men. His living room was filled with equipment from his screen-printing business.

Because there was no room in the living area, he directed me to his room, suggested I sit on the end of his bed and handed me the photos I wanted to see. While looking through them and asking him questions, I was handed a glass of wine. He said it was the last of the bottle and he wanted to finish it up. There was barely an inch of liquid, so I swallowed it in one gulp, handed him the glass, and returned my focus to the pictures in my hands.

My world began to tilt and other than a few dreamlike memories of sexual activity, I remember nothing until the following morning when he woke me, threw a towel at me, and ordered me to shower.

"This isn't a hotel," he said brusquely as he walked out of the room.

I was confused, and my arms and legs didn't seem to want to cooperate with me as I climbed out of bed, wrapped a towel around myself, and shuffled to the shower. My head didn't hurt with hangover, but my mind was filled with fog. Each time I lifted my arms, they felt heavy, as did my legs and feet. Something was wrong, but I didn't know what it was.

It had snowed during the night and as he drove me home during the early morning hours, he pulled into a mall parking lot and turned the car in circles, making donuts in the snow, the back part of the car swerving back and forth.

Several months later, a news program did a story about men going to Mexico and returning with a date rape drug. They described the symptoms after being dosed. They sounded quite familiar.

I didn't hear from him after that night and figured I had disappointed him somehow since he didn't want to go out again. A month later when my period didn't come I began to worry. I was always on time. Also, I had been taking "the pill" since I was eighteen years old. After another week without my period's appearance, I went to the doctor.

My whole world came crashing down around me—I was pregnant. It was a few days before I had the courage to call him and tell him he was going to be a father.

"Get an abortion," he said, and that was the last we spoke for a long time.

All I could see in this cold moment were the words rejected, failure, worthless, abandoned. I was the sum of these words.

When my parents split and divorced, a new pastor was assigned to our Methodist church. Rev. Guinn and his wife had a calling for youth, and they became a stabilizing force in my unstable life—almost like surrogate parents. Rev. Guinn liked to take youth out to lunch and for ice cream, but he also took us to hospitals and taught us to serve. I remember him taking me to the burn hospital in Boston to visit the children who were suffering unimaginable pain. Their faces lit when they saw him coming. A moment of love to fill in between the terrifying treatments they had to endure.

I had spent a great deal of time visiting hospitals with Rev. Guinn, but still did not know much about God. Somewhere in my mind I believed if I served or helped enough, that God would love me. I didn't believe my father loved me. How could I believe the almighty God could love me? When I found out I was pregnant, I told Rev. Guinn.

"Oh, dear baby," he said. "Your life is ruined. You need to get an abortion, so you don't destroy your life."

There it was. If a man of God believed I had ruined my life, then God must think the same. I am unlovable, a failure. In my head I had an image of the perfect ceramic figurine I was trying to be for God, smashed on the floor in a million pieces. Unfixable. A great disappointment.

I could not abort my baby. To me, it was a precious life. And even though it brought comments of embarrassment for having a child out of wedlock from some family members, I just could not kill the baby. I stopped going to church after my former Sunday school teacher's wife looked at my growing belly with disdain as I took my seat beside my grandmother in the pew.

This event reinforced that rejection and failure were inextricably linked to my identity and love confused itself with sex. I was unlovable, broken, unfixable, and no one would want me. I believed this to the core of my being. Yet in the midst of the pain, self-loathing, doubt, and accusations, one good thing came into my life—my daughter.

I hadn't yet learned that God intentionally chooses the foolish, the worthless, and the unwanted. I recently read Matt Bays' book, *Finding God in the Ruins*[5].

He quoted 1 Corinthians 1:27 (The Message) "Isn't it obvious that God deliberately chose men and women that the culture overlooks and exploits and abuses, chose the 'nobodies' to expose the hollow pretensions of the 'somebodies.'"

Then he wrote: "We measure pain and love from the day we are born. At times it feels the sands of pain are sifted so much heavier than the sands of love, and we forever wonder if it's because of something we've missed along the way or something we've done wrong. For many of us, it seems there is no such thing as grace. Most of us accept grace only after we have exhausted our options and realized that we will never be able to pay what we owe—and we are right. But grace is life, and it's all around us for the taking."

---

5   Matt Bays, *Finding God in the Ruins: How God Redeems Pain* (Colorado Springs, Colorado: David C. Cook 2016).

In my mind, there was no grace, no mercy, and no forgiveness. Everything I did was a disappointment. I was unlovable, unwanted, and worthless. I was broken.

But soon after my daughter's birth, God, in his infinite love, would reach down into my pain, extend mercy to me, forgive me, and make me into the very grace I thought was unavailable.

CHAPTER SIXTEEN

DAUGHTER OF THE KING

"You are [I am] a letter from Christ, the result of our ministry, written not with ink but with the spirit of the living God, not on tablets of stone but on tablets of human hearts."
2 Corinthians 3:3

Was I willing to send my baby daughter to die for others? That question rocked my world, flipped everything I knew on its head, and shook out the pain from the pockets of my heart, mind, and soul.

It was March 29, 1987. I was sitting in a little church in Connecticut listening to a woman named Joanne Sheptock preaching. It was the first time I heard that God loved us so much he sent his Son to die for us. It was a God moment, a time in which I realized I was loved, even with my failures and brokenness.

When I was pregnant with my daughter, Rev. Guinn introduced me to a young woman named Ruth. As a single mother, she was doing foster care for medically involved children. I was intrigued by her life because there was something different about her. I couldn't put my finger on it, but something kept drawing me closer and closer to her.

Ruth spoke a lot about God. I recall lying on a bed while pregnant, listening to her talk about this God, whom I believed would never accept me because I was too damaged to be accepted and loved. I would think, "Yeah, yeah, when is she going to stop talking about this God?"

At the time I was working as a bookkeeper for a private foster care and adoption agency. I had wanted to become a writer or teacher, but when my parents were in the middle of their divorce, my father refused to pay for college to study writing.

"You need something that will pay you well," he said. "Journalists have a bad reputation, and teachers don't earn enough money."

When I started college in the fall of 1982, I studied business financial management because that was what he wanted me to do. I hated it, but I was good at it. After that first year of college, because of other circumstances in my life, I began working full time and attending classes at night. Then I had to drop my studies after becoming pregnant with my daughter.

Ruth talked a lot about this woman Joanne Sheptock who had adopted about thirty children and fostered hundreds more, most of them with some sort of disability. I was fascinated by her story. When Ruth told me Joanne Sheptock would be speaking one Sunday in Connecticut, I decided to accompany her on the four-hour drive. I didn't go because I wanted to hear her speak, I went because I was curious about her. I wanted to find out why her life was so different from everyone else's.

That Sunday morning I sat in the back row with the window to the nursery, where my four-month-old daughter was being cared for, behind me. I listened as Joanne talked of her life and how God moved in it. She spoke of how much God loved us and how he wanted a relationship with us. Then she asked everyone in the room who had a child to raise their hands.

I raised mine.

"Do you love everyone who ever was, is now, and ever will be, enough to send your child to die for them?" she asked.

I pulled my arm down as fast as I could. I never would send my daughter to die for anyone.

"For God so loved the world," she said, "that he gave his one and only Son, that whoever believes in him shall not perish but have eternal life. He loves you so much he sent his Son to die for you. To pay all of your sins and give you righteousness."

It was as though I was sleep walking through lunch and the four-hour drive home. What Joanne said kept knocking on my heart. It was that mosquito bite that itches and itches and won't go away. I replayed her message over and over in my head while staring out the window on the drive home.

"Did God love me this much?" I wondered. "Even with all my failures, bad decisions, and brokenness?"

Sometime between seven and eight that night, just after I put my baby daughter to bed, the Holy Spirit reached down into the depths of my brokenness. The light and love of God flooded into my darkness.

I fell onto my knees, tears streaming down my face onto the carpet as I rocked back and forth receiving his love into my heart. I gave him my life that night in the basement studio apartment of my mother's house as my daughter slept in the crib. For the first time in my life, I knew I was completely loved, forgiven, and accepted—no, not accepted—chosen.

It would be easy to say everything changed at that moment, but it didn't. It would take almost thirty years on the journey with my Savior before I fully realized who I was in Christ. One could say my journey with the Lord began that night, when it began the day I was formed in my mother's womb.

When my daughter was fifteen months old, I answered God's call to care for special needs children in foster care. Everyone told me I couldn't do it. I was single, didn't own my own home, and I was too young. But I believed it when God said I could do all things through Christ who strengthens me. I clung to that Scripture so many times in my life, especially when someone told me I couldn't do something.

That was the thing about my faith: I believed what God said. I didn't fight with understanding: I just believed. He would supply all my needs and I could do all things.

I did become a foster mother, alongside my stepsister Allison. We both received the calling and pooled our resources, so we could become foster parents.

I left my job, collected my comp time, vacation, and sick pay and set out to serve God as a foster parent. We took the training classes and waited . . . and waited. Nothing happened. No children came.

One night a week before our money ran out and we would find ourselves homeless and without jobs with our daughters—Allison also had a daughter "out of wedlock" just like I did—my spirit reached a new low point as the fear of failure rose inside me. That night I sat on my porch in the rain, smoked a cigarette, and yelled at God.

"You told me to do this!" I shouted to the darkness above me as rain hit my face, joining the tears of frustration making their own descent on my cheeks. I felt betrayed.

"You told me to do foster care! Everyone said we couldn't do it and I told them you said we could do all things! Here we are, and the money is going to run out. If we fail, I will tell them all you are a liar!"

Yes, I told God I would tell everyone he was a liar.

"I believed what you said!" I continued shouting as my wet clothes began to stick to my body. "This is impossible for me to do on my own. Everyone has said this. I told them you were doing this, and I refuse to believe you won't!"

A few days later the first call came, and so did my first foster child. Then another call came and another and another. For almost eight years I cared for broken children, those nobody wanted to care for or were afraid to take. I became mother to more than thirty children and I told the world God had done this. Yes, I could do all things through Christ who strengthened me. Allison and I lived together for two years, each caring for our own foster children until we were financially able to go it on our own.

My friend Ruth was patient with my questions about God and brought me to her church. For seven years I attended that spirit-filled church, learning everything I could about God. I was a sponge that could not suck up all I wanted—needed—to learn and apply to my life.

It was at that church that I met Fred. He was an usher and was attending the first year of a two-year Bible school the church offered. He helped me with my children each time I came to church.

Fred and I became friends. When he wanted to date, I was thrilled. The words I frequently heard from my father, "Who is going to want you with all those kids?" haunted me. But Fred wanted me. He said so, even with all those kids.

Those of us who are broken in our identity frequently make bad decisions because our decisions are based on the negative things others say to us. This happens frequently with domestic violence victims. The moment they are told someone wants them, or loves them, they jump into a relationship because they don't believe anyone could love them. This was where I was. Because of it, I made several bad decisions during the next several years of my life.

Shortly after beginning a relationship with Fred, I discovered he was on parole. He had been imprisoned for sexually molesting children and had been on a prison release program when I met him. Because of good behavior, his work in the church, and his enrollment in the Bible school, he was granted parole.

I broke up with Fred, and another dark and scary period of my life ensued. He began stalking me. Neighbors told me they saw Fred outside my apartment, watching my home, and writing down the license plates of the cars in the parking lot. When I went to the grocery store with the children, I encountered him lurking in the aisles. When one of my foster children had surgery, hospital nurses told me he had been seen in the hallways outside our room.

I told the pastor and his wife what was going on and they didn't believe me. Fred was a good man, they said. He was doing well in Bible school and was helping in the church. They refused to believe he was stalking and terrorizing me.

The dinosaur nightmares returned, and another nightmare began of Fred breaking into my house and killing me while I slept. I was terrified. I had to sleep with the television on because any noise I heard kept me from sleeping. I placed furniture in front of the doors before going to bed, hoping it would stop him and alert me should he try and break in.

One night near midnight, as I opened the back door to the porch where I stored equipment for one of my foster babies, I came face-to-face with him. He had gotten into the back stairwell and had been peeking through my kitchen curtains, watching what I was doing. I opened the back door and we were nose-to-nose. I slammed the door and flipped the latch. I didn't sleep at all that night. In the morning I called the pastor and his wife at the church. But again, they didn't believe me.

This continued for five months. Sleepless nights and days of constant looking over my shoulder became my life. Stalking does serious damage to a person. It brings a fear so profound that it is almost impossible to shake, and you don't feel safe in your own home. Even after it ended, I still slept with the television on for years and still feel uncomfortable with people being able to see me in my house through windows.

Because I had severely impaired children, the state gave me a nurse three times a week for eight hours to give me respite. One day I came home from shopping and the nurse told me the pastor's wife had called. I was told she sounded upset and wanted me to immediately call her when I returned.

I called the pastor's wife.

"Is everything all right?" she asked, a sense of fear and urgency in her voice. "The police showed up at the church with an arrest warrant for Fred. They cuffed him in the hallway and took him away."

She didn't know why he had been arrested and said she feared he had done something to me or the children. I later learned he had abused his own six-year-old son.

In the aftermath of the "Fred" situation, the words "Who would want you?" returned. Other words like, "We are embarrassed you have children and are not married," joined the taunting in my spirit. The desire to be loved and wanted, even though I knew God loved me, began to consume my life. I didn't understand that his love was enough. It didn't help me at all that not only did I hear these words echoing in my mind, but I also heard them from people who should have loved me.

Again, I was a failure.

Then I met Donnie. He was a likeable guy, a happy prankster whose smile made everyone feel at ease. When I met him, he was living with his mother in the house next to mine because he was separated from his wife. She wanted to divorce him, he said, because of his back injury.

He began to hang out with me, watching movies, bringing food and other things to help me out. One of his hobbies was driving around neighborhoods on trash days collecting metal and other things he could sell. He found lots of furniture and toys for the children I had in my care.

When his divorce came through we began dating. Here was a man (again) who said he wanted me in his life. And he really did. He also began attending church with me and received Christ as his Savior. Then he proposed.

Again I was able to shout back at those haunting words. Someone loves me! I am wanted! I am of value!

The wedding plans were in full swing, invitations sent. About two months before the wedding, Donnie wanted to have sex. I wanted to wait until we were married, but that night in January I consented.

A few weeks later I discovered I was pregnant. Shame returned. Donnie was excited to become a father again—he had four other children through three other women. We sought counsel and were told to speak with my pastor, the same pastor who did not believe me when I told him Fred was stalking me.

A shiver of cold hit me from the top of my head, rolling down to the tips of my toes when the pastor said we should cancel the wedding and wait until after the baby was born to get married. He wanted us to be sure we were not getting married because I was pregnant.

The cold terror of failure gripped me. Yet another pastor said I failed. Yet again I would have a baby without being married. Donnie agreed with the pastor and the feelings of not being wanted gripped my heart. I was so shaken and upset by the new turn of events that I refused to make any of the calls to cancel the wedding.

Throughout the pregnancy, Donnie remained by my side. I thought he would leave. After our son was born, he proposed again, and we were married when my son was eight months old. When we returned from our honeymoon, everything changed. Donnie stopped going to church and was barely ever home.

It was then I discovered he was addicted to drugs. I knew he had a back injury and took a lot of medicine. But once we moved in together, I noticed he had numerous bottles of Percocet prescribed by various doctors. When I confronted him about it, he said the pain was bad and doctors didn't give him enough meds.

Then I discovered he was also buying the drugs on the street. A friend would call, and Donnie would leave. When he returned I would find him in the bedroom or the kitchen crushing the Percocet in a paper and snorting it. I didn't know what to do.

I figured if I took the money away from him, I could at least get him to stop buying the drugs on the street. I reworked our budget and gave him an allowance. I did not know that no one can control an addict. I was young, naive, and in a panic.

He maxed out our credit cards, taking out two hundred to four hundred dollars each time to buy drugs. Then, when we had no more money to access, he began selling drugs. He would buy twenty pills at five dollars each then sell ten at ten dollars each.

I couldn't take it anymore. One day as we drove in our van with all the children to visit one of our foster children in the hospital, he pulled the van over and got out. He walked across the street in the rain, spoke to a man in a parked car, bought drugs, and returned to the van.

I was furious. He had just committed a drug deal in front of me and the children. We argued all the way to the hospital and again on the way home.

"I am not doing anything illegal," he said. "They are prescriptions."

"You're a drug dealer," I told him. "You have to stop!"

Failure screamed at me in the dark recesses of my mind.

"You make bad decisions," it told me. "Who wants you? Only a drug dealer and addict would want you."

Worthless put in its two cents, and even though I was walking with the Lord, I was still broken and stumbling around in the darkness into which my life had fallen. I was consumed by words that whirled in my head.

"You're worthless, unlovable, broken, a failure—again!"

I researched programs to get Donnie help and told him he had to decide: me and God and the children . . . or the drugs. He said he would try rehab.

We found an in-patient program his insurance would cover, giving him four weeks of detox followed by five weeks of pain management therapy.

Just short of two weeks into his detox, I was in the kitchen making lunch when I heard the front door open and Donnie walked into the kitchen with a big smile on his face.

"They let me out," he said. "I finished the detox early and there is no space in the rehab for another week or so."

Something inside me, most likely the Holy Spirit, told me he was lying. After he dumped his bags on our bed upstairs, he informed me he was going out to meet one of his friends and would be back for dinner.

As soon as he pulled out of the driveway, I called the hospital.

"He walked out of the program," the counselor told me. "He refused to work with us and walked out. You need to convince him to come back."

The word "betrayed" screamed its way around my head as tears of frustration and fear filled my eyes. I ran upstairs, grabbed his bags, brought them down, and threw them onto the porch with all the strength I had. Then I bolted the doors.

He returned a few hours later and banged on the door.

"You lied to me!" I shouted through the door. "I called the hospital and they told me you walked out. Me and God and the kids, or your drugs!"

I walked away from the door and sat on the couch. I heard him pick up his bags and mumble something as he walked down the porch steps. The next morning he called me from the hospital and told me he was working the program. He promised he would do it for us and the children.

About ten days later, when I returned home from shopping, I saw the light blinking on the answering machine in the living room. A sense of foreboding curled up my spine. I pushed the message play button and heard the counselor from the hospital telling me they had kicked Donnie out of rehab. He was not only not cooperating with his own recovery, but he was also impeding the recovery of the other patients. They told me to not let Donnie back in the house.

I cried. Donnie loved the drugs more than us. I locked the doors and sat on the couch, feeling lost as the word "failure" crept back in, taunting and torturing me. It wasn't long before I heard a voice at the door. It was Donnie, his happy voice saying he had finished the program and been released early.

Our first anniversary had been only days before, uncelebrated because he was in rehab. I had spent that night alone on the couch praying for my husband to be freed from addiction, so we could have a fruitful marriage and life together. I begged God to give him the strength to be the man of God he was made to be.

I saw my life and marriage crashing around me. I thought a life with God, serving him as I was with the foster care, studying the Word every night, attending church regularly, would be easier. It wasn't supposed to be this hard; it wasn't supposed to be filled with failure.

Replete with resignation and thoughts of failure, I rose from the couch, walked to the front door and stood face-to-face with my husband. It took every ounce of strength to confront him.

"Me and God and the kids, or the drugs," I said. "You lied to me again. You didn't even try. You made your choice."

I pulled the curtain over the window and went back to the couch, where I cried for hours. For three nights he slept in his car in our driveway, hoping it would convince me to let him in. I refused. His mother called repeatedly to tell me what a bad wife I was and that I was ruining their family reputation because I was making him sleep on the streets. A couple of months later, I moved to another city and began divorce proceedings.

The letters "F" for failure, "W" for worthless, "U" for unwanted, and "B" for broken were blazoned upon my heart. I was a FWUB! The story of my life. I was a nobody. My life was one string of failures after another.

Sexually abused, raped and pregnant, single mother, married to a drug addict and dealer, now a single, divorced woman.

I was living proof that all the things spoken over me were true.

It couldn't get worse. But it did.

After I moved to another apartment in another city, and while my divorce was becoming final, people at the church began to counsel me, or rather, give me their opinions.

"A Christian wife would make her husband choose her over the drugs," they would say.

Now I was a failure as a Christian *and* a wife.

A few months after moving to the new apartment, I met Barry. He was sweet and loving. But he was also an alcoholic. I believe I went into that relationship ignoring his alcoholism because I believed no one better would want me. My life was living proof that the only men who wanted anything to do with me were "mess ups" just like me.

It wasn't long before Barry became abusive and I became the target for his abuse. Accusations about the clothes I wore attracting other men, questions about where I went, who I spoke with, and what I did were fired at me daily. I began restructuring my days and activities, so Barry wouldn't become angry with me.

When he became physically violent, I went to his uncle for advice. Barry saw me talking to him and assumed I was having an affair. He ran up to us, grabbed me by the throat, pushed me against the wall, all the while screaming horrible words I cannot even remember. The only thing that existed in that moment was fear and the pressure of his hands around my throat. It took four men to pull him off me and save my life.

The police were involved, and a restraining order was put into place. However, after a few weeks he started coming to the door to speak with me, his manner sweet as it was before. He promised me things would be different if we got back together. I believed him.

At this time my finances were in the gutter because my husband had left me with a lot of debt because of his drug use. I invited Barry back into my life because he promised to not be violent anymore and began helping me with the rent because I didn't have enough money to pay it. Aggressors like to make their victims dependent on them. I allowed Barry to do that to me.

Fear and constant harassment pulled me down so far, I entertained the thought of suicide.

One night I sat on my bed crying. I felt as though I was being sucked down into a black vortex. Suicide offered its cure. I just wanted the pain to stop.

"Jesus help me," I screamed into the darkness that was swallowing me.

Something happened. As I fell into the dark vortex, I saw a hand reaching down to me. I reached up, the hand took mine and suddenly I felt peace. The hand slowly pulled me up out of the vortex and I saw my savior. He pulled me into his arms and held me. I curled up in his arms and stayed there all night.

Relief came like a flood over me, redeeming me. But I wasn't quite ready for God to rescue and restore me. I was still with Barry because I needed him both to love me and I needed his financial help. I opened a small bookkeeping service, helping small businesses with their accounting needs. I had also begun pursuing my dream of becoming a writer.

At this time, home computers were coming into vogue. I joined the America Online Writer's Club and created its first online poetry community. I met writers who had been published, made many friends, and received encouragement to write. I believe the greatest love and encouragement I have ever received in my life up to that point came through a group of female writers. We called ourselves "The Sistahs." They believed in me when I didn't believe in myself.

The situation with Barry came to a head one night. My daughter and I had been out looking at new cars and I had bought one. But as we did the paperwork, I realized the time. Barry was off work, and should he come to the house and I not be there, I would pay for it that night. I realized in that moment how much control he had over my life.

That night he came home late and drunk. Insults flew around the apartment like mashed potatoes in a food fight. He screamed insults and accusations and I cried and defended myself. I had never thought about the impact it had on my children until my nine-year-old daughter stood up to him in the living room. I will never forget watching my tiny fair-haired daughter stand up to a drunk when I could not.

"Barry, I don't like it when you yell at my mother!" she screamed at him, her face red, and her tiny finger pointing at him like a mother chastising her child. "It's not right! She didn't do anything wrong! You are drunk and mean!"

Watching her gave me the courage to make a change. I threw him out of the house that night and committed to God that it would be "me and God and my kids."

During the following years God marked me, or I realized I had been marked by God all along. Real change began to grow in my life like a sprout fresh out of the ground.

Every time I went through something, people would ask me how I got through it.

"How did you get through a rape and becoming pregnant?"

"How did you get through a husband who was a drug addict and dealer? A divorce?"

"Being a single mom? Being stalked? How did you get through being a victim of domestic violence?"

Each time they asked, I replied, "By the grace of God."

One day a friend who was not a Christian told me he was tired of me saying "the grace of God" and said everyone should just call me Gracie. I don't remember when this happened, but it was sometime during 1995 and 1996.

Before I knew it, I was no longer Robin. I was Gracie.

It was then the Lord gave me 1 Corinthians 15:10 (NIV), "But by the grace of God I am what I am, and his grace to me was not without effect."

God had taken the broken pieces of my life, the failures, the bad decisions, and unlovable moments and made something beautiful out of it. He took every part of me and redeemed me. I was on a new path, in a new life, I had been renewed. I left everything behind, packed up my children and moved away from the Boston area to the South. I started a new life with my children, pursued my writing career, and went back to school for my degree, which included English and communications, as well as criminal justice studies.

After about three years of living in Alabama with my mantra "just me and God and my kids," I met Lee, a pastor from northern Alabama. We met on the internet in a Christian chat room when I was looking for advice on a situation. He gave me the advice I needed, and I thought that would be it. But he continued to communicate with me.

At first we were just friends. I liked it that way. Things were going well for me for the first time in my life, and I didn't want another man to ruin things. I didn't trust myself to let one in since I had made so many bad choices in my past.

But he pursued. We talked for hours on the phone because he lived in northern Alabama and I in the southern part. Finally, we arranged a meeting. I was driving my son to Atlanta airport with my daughter, so he could go on his summer visit with his father in Boston. Lee and I decided it would be a good time to meet.

I can still remember him standing against his car door in the parking lot of the gas station off the exit. I even asked him for his identification to prove he was who he said he was, even though I had already done a thorough investigation on him. I was nervous about meeting a man with my daughter by my side. Who knew what could happen?

We first visited at his house, had some iced tea and talked. Then he took me to his parents' home for a family barbecue. It was a Saturday afternoon. He had told them about me only a couple of days before. They were a bit wary of me and my daughter, but we all had a great time.

That evening we sat with his parents, watched television, and talked. The funny thing about that night was he left me with his parents and went home. It was the right thing to do being a pastor and us both being Christians. But I must confess I was nervous. I came to meet this man and he left me with his parents for the night. Waking up and having coffee and breakfast with strangers before we went to church to hear Lee preach was a bit awkward for us all. We have laughed about that for years.

During the next months, Lee wanted to become more than friends, but I was afraid. I was a FWUB. God would not let a FWUB be a girlfriend of a pastor. I was unworthy. I feared that if I kissed him, God would toss down a lightning bolt and strike me dead on the spot. I liked my life how it was without drama or problems.

I prayed about Lee and told the Lord I was unworthy to be a pastor's girlfriend, as pictures of lightning bolts were in my head. But in the quiet, I heard the Lord whisper.

"It is these very things that make you able to be with him. Your brokenness means you understand suffering. I can use that. A pastor's wife needs to understand pain, so she can help others heal. You know what it is like to be abused and raped, pregnant by that rape, to struggle as a single mother."

Eleven months later we were married.

The night he proposed—Christmas Eve—he was so nervous his entire body trembled. When he showed me the ring and knelt to pop the question, I held out my hand to stop him and asked if I could ask him a question first.

"You are not only marrying me," I said. "You are also marrying my children. I need to know if you will be the father they never had."

He said yes; I said yes, and the rest is history. We have been married more than eighteen years, and he has been an amazing father and husband. Not only has he been an amazing father to Ashley and Dominic, but also to everyone who has come under our care. Hundreds of children—and adults—call him Papi.

I had been walking a road marked with suffering, living a life of failure mostly because I didn't understand who I was in Christ. I believed all the things that had been spoken over me. God's grace came into my life and transformed me. His mercy poured over me like fresh oil from heaven.

I still struggle a bit with my identity and who I am in Christ, but since I took that turn in the road my life has changed. Yes, I have walked through storm after storm since then and faced death in the work I do, but God is continually transforming me into Gracie. My life is a living testimony of his grace in me. All that I have become and done is evidence of his grace in me.

When I look back on my life, all I can see is grace.

Matt Bays says it perfectly in his book, *Finding God in the Ruins:*

"I've never seen myself as a worthy representative of God because too much happened to me as a child, and my doubt has often left me feeling entirely inadequate. Oh, there are times I fully expect people to find out the truth about me: that I'm a fraud. And maybe it's true—maybe I am damaged goods. Maybe . . . my only rescue is to be so wrapped up with God that my whole life belongs to him . . . Could it be that for all the darkness within me, and for all the brokenness . . . God put his song of dark and light in me and I've been singing it all this time—singing the song I was always meant to sing?

A song that's honest and raw. A song of healing and pain. A song of love and hate. A song of hope and a song of doubt."

I am still on this journey of finding out who I am in Christ. I don't think I will fully come to the end of discovering who Gracie is until I am face-to-face with him. But I am who I am by his grace. And I am living my life in a manner that his grace extended to and put in me will not be without effect.

There is a saying floating on the internet which I have hanging on the wall in my office. I do not know its origin, but it says:

"I am the daughter of a King who is not moved by the world for my God is with me and goes before me. I do not fear because I am his."

Another one I found recently says:

"On my darkest days, when I feel inadequate, unloved and unworthy, I remember whose daughter I am, and I straighten my crown."

Through all the challenges I have overcome with him, through all the things I have learned as I have grown closer to him, I have discovered that I am not defined by my past, what people say about me, or by my mistakes. I can choose who has the right to define me and I choose that only God has the right to define who I am.

I am GRACE, daughter of the King of Kings, Lord of all the Earth, and Master of all creation.

I have been established, anointed, and sealed by God.

THE JOURNEY MATTERS

"And let us run with perseverance
the race marked out for us."
Hebrews 12:1

Sometimes the most profound revelations come from the most unexpected places.

After writing a report to our new colonel about our work and finishing my quarterly report to our ministry leaders, I was resting and watching a television program called *Grey's Anatomy*.

Surgeons were confounded by a huge tumor behind a woman's liver. To save her life during surgery they had to be creative and came up with the idea to remove her liver, do the surgery and put her liver back. It had never been done before and they had only seconds to decide because she was crashing. They took the risk and saved her life.

At the end of the show, as the doctors were celebrating their victory, the voice-over commentary said:

"When people climb a mountain, they always take a picture celebrating their victory. Their faces are always smiling. But no one ever takes pictures during the arduous climb or at the moments the hikers believe they cannot make it any further."

Hence the focus is always on the achievement. Not on the journey.

This profoundly struck me.

I thought about the quarterly report, which requested information about ministry activities, major ministry events in the last quarter, major ministry events planned in the next quarter, praise reports such as salvations, baptisms and answered prayer, and lastly prayer requests.

Previously I wrote a report for one of our church sponsors who wanted a count of lives saved and if the church was persecuted for its ministry. When I write reports for the authorities in Honduras, they want to know how many people attended events or the outcome of missions.

Reporting victories and accomplishments is important in many ways, such as in compiling statistics and determining effectiveness. But I always sensed there was something missing, as I did when I wrote that report. I did not know what it was until I heard that statement on *Grey's Anatomy*.

The truth is, I can't tell you how many people accepted salvation, although there have been numerous salvations and baptisms. I can tell you how many cases we handled, how many victims we ministered to, and how many people to whom we preached.

I can't tell you the church is persecuted, but I can tell you I am persecuted for this ministry service and sometimes at risk of being murdered because of it. I can tell you that we plan to hold events in churches and schools and with leaders, but those events are not the journey.

The journey is as important as the achievements because without the journey there are no achievements. That goes for what I am doing now, which would not exist if not for the journey I had to walk to get here.

Because of our ministry, we are well known. People, including police officers, lawyers, judges, the media—everyone—talks about our ministry.

The telephone number for the ministry is better known than the telephone for the police. Why? Because they know that in Christ we bring hope.

One Saturday years ago, I was lonely at the mission and went to Talanga to check on the office. Nothing was happening there, so I sat on the bench in front of the police station to watch people. A man I had never seen before came up to me, called me by name, and told me he was a truck driver and needed my help.

He said that while driving his truck into the mountains, he came across a woman carrying a boy who was six years old but was the size of a toddler. He said the boy was severely disabled. He gave the woman and her child a ride to where they lived in the mountains of Majada Verde. He was delivering supplies and couldn't bear to think of her carrying that child for four hours.

During the drive he learned the woman's husband had abandoned her, the boy, and her fourteen-year-old daughter to live with another woman. She said her husband was a drunk and never gave her money to support her children. Because of this, she took her daughter out of school and sent her to Talanga to work as a domestic. But her husband often took her daughter's pay for his drinking.

The man told me he didn't know what to do to help this family. He knew about our ministry and hoped we could help him help them. We talked about what we could do, and I praised him for being a caring human being and told him that God would bless him.

Another day, after spending five hours in praise and worship to overcome the stress I was feeling about the challenges we were facing, my telephone rang. It was a young woman whom I have never met, and she also called me by name. She told me she was pregnant, had two children, and her husband was seeing another woman. Crying, she said she felt she was alone in this world and asked if I knew of a place where she could go.

I talked with her about family, and we agreed to contact her brother. Maybe he and his wife could help her. I told her she was not alone. God was with her. I then shared with her how sometimes I felt lonely and how everyone thinks I am this strong woman who never has any problems.

I told her I was just like everyone else, and with Easter the next day I was missing my family and was feeling lonely. I shared with her how I spent the previous five hours in praise and worship and God filled me up. How he let me know I was not alone and through him I could overcome any situation. I told her I had been a single mother for twelve years and God helped me through it. I told her he was with her every day . . . every step.

I didn't pray the prayer of salvation with her. She said she was already saved and named the church she attended. She agreed God was with her and said after our call she would listen to praise music and praise God until her oppression lifted. She also asked me to keep her phone number and, if I ever were lonely, to call her.

Every day my phone rings; sometimes only once or twice and sometimes more than forty times. Almost every caller is a desperate life seeking hope. My job—my journey—is to take the time to minister to whomever is at the other end of the line, to counsel, love, comfort, and support the person crying out for help. More than 90 percent of the people who call me I never meet. Some days it is overwhelming; I want the telephone to stop ringing.

When I go to the grocery store, children smile and point at me and whisper, "That's Gracie, no?" Or people cautiously approach me and say, "Can I ask you a question?" or "Can you give me some counsel?" They touch my arm in the street and ask for a moment; they approach me as I exit my car. Then they proceed to tell me about their suffering, asking for help, hope, a way out of the darkness.

One night, years ago, I sat in my living room, lonely because my husband was in the United States raising funds. It was either New Year's or Valentine's

Day. My phone rang. A woman was on the line; she said she lived in Talanga and wanted to thank us for all we do.

I asked her what she needed.

"Nothing," she said. "I only called to say thank you and tell you I pray for you every day."

I'd be lying if I said I didn't cry, but they weren't tears of sadness, they were tears of joy.

Another night my phone rang. A male voice on the other end said a man had just shot a young boy in the street in Pedernal, a mountain community an hour from us, and they needed help. I happened to be at the police station and sent Officer Sanchez with my cellphone to the colonel, who dispatched a *patrulla* to the village. They saved the boy's life and arrested the man who shot him.

I called the man the next day and asked why he called me instead of the police.

"We didn't know the number for the police, but had your number from the radio show," he said. "We also have the fliers you left when you spoke to all the students and parents in our community and we knew you'd get us help."

Several years ago a police officer in La Ermita told me about a woman in our village on the verge of death. The woman's mother had appealed to police for help because the family was too poor to call for an ambulance.

In Honduras, you must buy gas for the ambulance before it takes you to the hospital.

The woman, in her early twenties, had suffered a nervous breakdown after the birth of a child and had been in bed for fifteen days without eating or drinking in hundred-degree weather. The police officer asked for our help.

I called the Red Cross in Talanga. I asked if they could take the woman to the hospital in Tegucigalpa the following day when I would have access to money to pay for the trip.

"Let's go get her now and you can pay us tomorrow," they said.

The ambulance arrived at our mission and, along with police, we accompanied it to her home. She was taken to Tegucigalpa and her life was saved. A couple of years later, as we walked with a mission team through the village one morning, distributing bags of food and praying for people, we encountered the same woman. She was healthy and doing well.

She thanked us for helping her, and I told her that Jesus loved her. I shared his story and the plan of salvation. Right there, in the heat of mid-morning sun, hands held through bushes over a barbed-wire fence, she received Jesus as her Savior.

We spoke with her afterward about finding a church and getting baptized. She didn't want to wait. She wanted us to baptize her that same day. I explained we had plans to go into Talanga and go door-to-door praying for people and handing out food, the same task that had brought us to her door. We wouldn't be back at the mission until around four in the afternoon. We hugged over the fence and went on our way.

Returning to the mission a couple hours before dark, we found her sitting on the hillside in front of our gate with her mother. She was excited and ready to be baptized. Joyfully, the missionaries gathered in the center of the yard where Lee and another pastor stood, each with two five-gallon buckets of water. (We didn't have a cistern or baptismal.) We said a prayer, poured the water over her, baptizing her, and we all hugged and cried.

I later learned that the two women had waited more than two hours for us to arrive.

Then there was a midnight call from the Red Cross informing me of a man who was critically injured in a car wreck and was going to die if not taken to the hospital in Tegucigalpa. Neither he nor his family had money to put gas in the ambulance. Could we help?

The ambulance arrived at our door twenty minutes later with the patient. I handed the driver 500 lempiras ($25) for gasoline and prayed over the patient as the Red Cross attendant wrote out a receipt. The ambulance pulled away, sirens screaming and lights flashing as they disappeared down the village road.

If you are injured in Honduras, there is no guarantee an ambulance will come. If it does, the patient, or his family, must provide enough gasoline for the ambulance to get to the hospital and back. No money, no gas. No gas, no trip to the hospital.

Marale is a remote mountain community nestled in a valley surrounded by mountaintops, a two-hour drive north of our ministry. There are about nine thousand people in the county, which is filled mostly by mountains and farms. It is one of the poorest regions of Francisco Morazán. We coordinated with a mission group from a church in Guntersville, Alabama, and with the mayor of the village, Teresa Espinoza, to help a community of sixteen families rebuild their homes damaged in an earthquake.

The residents were supposed to help each other and work with the Americans, but they weren't. The families sat in their yards watching the Americans work on the first homes being repaired, waiting for the missionaries to commence work on their own.

I walked from house to house telling the residents they needed to help with the repairs of all sixteen homes for the project to be completed in the five days available for the project. But they refused, saying they wouldn't help with repairs on their neighbors' homes because their neighbors would do nothing once their own homes were fixed. They would be nowhere to be found.

I remember standing in their yards preaching the Word of God to these villagers as they sat in plastic chairs among the ruins of their half-collapsed homes. They had gone only as far as removing all the tiles from their roofs, stacking them on the ground and removing all the broken beams, considering this to be their contribution to the repair project.

As I explained that God wants us to help each other and will bless us if we do, I charged them to read the Word of God every day in their homes and told them it would change their lives. It was then I discovered none of the adults could read. I was dumbfounded, the wind had been knocked right out of me.

How could they grow spiritually if no one could read a Bible? What could I do to get them to understand that if they worked together they could achieve anything? How could I, in the short time I had, teach them that God would bless them if they helped others in the midst of their suffering? How was I going to persuade them to help each other so the project could be completed?

A group of chickens caught my eye. They were fighting over an ear of corn at the corner of a mud-and-stick-framed house. I picked up an ear of corn and held it up to them. I knew they understood farming because they were all farmers.

"If this is my ear of corn," I said, "and we are both hungry, and I say to you that I cannot share this ear with you because it is all I have, and then I eat it, what do I have left?"

"Nothing," they said.

"We are both still hungry and we both have nothing," I added. They nodded.

I then related the story of Jesus and the widow's offering.

"Jesus and his disciples were standing at the back of a church one day in a village much like the one we are standing in now. The pastor had just delivered a sermon about how our God is a God of harvest and he blesses those who give to, share with, and serve others in the midst of their own need. There was an air of excitement when the time came to take up the offering.

A man with fancy clothes arose, proudly walked up to the altar, and threw a thousand lempiras into the offering plate. Everyone gasped and clapped at such a great gesture and grand donation."

I paused momentarily before continuing.

"Then a widow slowly stood up and grabbed her cane. She hobbled ever so slowly up the aisle toward the altar," I said, acting out the hobbling of an old woman. "Everyone held their breath, expecting something big to happen. The widow continued slowly, step by step, until she finally stood before the offering plate. The crowd leaned forward as the widow pulled out her little bag from under her shawl and reached inside.

"Her hand came out. 'Clink!' She had dropped a coin, worth a mere fifty *centavos*, into the plate. The crowd was disappointed and began whispering about such a cheap donation. Even the disciples at the back of the room commented on the small gift.

"But Jesus told them that God would give a bigger blessing to the widow than he would to the rich man. Those who heard him speak this were shocked and thought Jesus was crazy. But Jesus told them what the man had given was nothing to him because he had millions of lempiras. It was like pocket change to him. The widow had given all that she had."

I then held up the cobb for them all to see. Everyone was watching intently. I continued.

"If I have this last ear of corn and pull out ten of the kernels and plant them in the ground, and then I eat the rest of the ear, what do I have left?"

They all responded saying I would have ten plants of corn grow out of the ground.

"Right. And when those stalks grow, and the corn becomes mature, I should have three to five ears of corn from each stalk. That would be maybe thirty to fifty ears of corn. And then I take ten kernels from each of them to plant and would have three hundred or more stalks with three to five ears of corn on each of them.

"This is what God does. We give out of our own need for the benefit of others and he blesses us with more than we had in the beginning." I looked around at the villagers sitting before me. "If all of you in the village work together, everyone's home will be repaired. But if everyone sits here watching the others work, waiting for the Americans to get to their house, the week will end with only a few houses repaired."

I could see by the looks in their eyes the idea was sinking into their brains. However, I was still frustrated that none of the adults could read. I asked God what to do, and how I could help them.

"And a little child will lead them," a whisper in my spirit.

Looking around at the children, I asked if any of them could read. A young boy about ten years old said that he could read. I gave him a Bible and told him that he was responsible for reading God's Word to his family and the others. With pride he promised me he would read to them every day.

The next day the people were all working together. When the Americans left at the end of the week, all but one home was finished. It was the widow's home—go figure.

"We are leaving the supplies for the widow's house," I said to the residents gathered around us to see us off. "I expect you all to finish it. I will be back the next week to make sure it is done."

It was two weeks before I had the chance to return and check on their work. Their village of sixteen families, Terrero Grande, was just outside the town of Marale unreachable by vehicle on a narrow path at the end of a dirt road. During our mission team's work there, we had to haul sand, tin, bags of cement, and other supplies on the backs of horses and donkeys as well as our own. The first day the villagers and Americans had to widen the path with machetes to bring the materials up to the homes.

I walked into the widow's yard, through her banana and other fruit trees and bushes covered with flowers. When I looked at the front of the mud-brick house and saw nothing had been done, my heart sank. I heard men talking and moving about on the other side of another patch of bushes and banana trees. I called out to them.

Two men appeared from behind the bushes and smiled when they saw me, excitement filling their faces.

"Why hasn't anyone worked on the widow's roof?" I asked.

They looked at each other then back at me.

"Well, *Licenciada*," one began, formally addressing me with a title meant for people who have graduated from university. "We evaluated her house and what needed to be done and realized it was too damaged to repair. The whole structure is leaning and about to fall."

"Come see! We're building her a new house!" the other interjected, excited to show me the work they had done.

They guided me to another small clearing where I saw a foundation with cement block walls going up for a little two-room house.

"My family down the road is taking care of the widow until we finish her house," one of the men said.

The men whose houses had been repaired were donating one day a week for the work on the house—and other projects. During my two-week absence, they had inspected other houses on the edge of their village and further up the mountain. When they found a house that needed work, they spoke with the mayor, who provided the materials, and they provided the labor for the repairs.

They also told me many of them would gather in one of the homes while the boy read the Bible to them.

I could not speak. I stood there staring at the men and the house they were building. The men and women of Terrero Grande understood what we had tried to teach them. I felt awe in the presence of God's work.

Several months later Honduras suffered another major crisis. Torrential rains fell, prompting mudslides that destroyed villages and roads, and damaged homes throughout the country. We worked with police and mayors on damage assessments and, because we were the only ones with internet access, we sent the reports to COPECO, the Honduran counterpart of FEMA, every night around midnight.

The only damage in Terrero Grande were the PVC pipes that brought water from the mountain springs down into their village. Not one of their homes was damaged. Even more remarkable, their county—Marale—had been one of the most damaged in the northern half of our state.

Their neighbors' homes suffered damage, but they did not. When we spoke to them while delivering relief supplies with the police, the villagers asked if we could donate the materials, so they could repair their water system. The mayor, who was with us, said another community had its water system destroyed.

We agreed to buy the supplies for both systems and the men of Terrero Grande said they would provide the labor to rebuild both systems. The people from that village continued working together on other homes with the help of their mayor.

They got it! And when disaster came, their area being hit hardest, not one of their homes was harmed. This they knew was a sign from God, that he was faithful to his word.

These are some of the moments along the journey when God shows up and changes lives forever. There are frustrating days, good days, and days in which we make significant progress. Then there are other days when everything falls apart.

It is like a photo of climbers at the summit of Mount Everest, the victory at the end. But no one takes a picture—or shows it if they do—of the time they fell into the river after they slipped on a rock. No one takes the picture of the five thousand times they need to sit down and rest because the journey was so arduous. Or of the moment someone trips and twists their ankle, or when their tent comes off the tent pegs in the blizzard near the summit and they find themselves rolling down the mountain.

These dark moments along the journey are turning points: we decide to surrender . . . or to press on.

In Honduras, moments like these are part of the journey: dealing with pain, grief, injustice, corruption, and sometimes threats of death.

Sometimes it takes the form of climbing a mountain, pushing coffee leaf branches out of my face, swatting mosquitoes off my arms, and eating only beans and tortillas because there is nothing else on a mission to recover a kidnapped child.

Some days I am so tired I wonder if I can continue. Other days I am full of joy and energy. And yet other days the frustrations beat at me like waves on the shore during a storm. At times I feel forgotten by friends and family in the United States who are busy with their own lives.

Sometimes at midnight, I am holding a bloodied woman or a child in my arms telling them it will be all right after they have been raped or severely beaten.

It is sitting with a family who witnessed their daughter/mother hacked to death by a man with a machete and returning to their home a couple of days later. It is talking to them on the phone every day to get them through this horrible event.

This is the journey. I can't count how many lives we have touched . . . or saved . . . or how many people we baptized. I can tell you that every day we are ministering hope and God's Word to the hopeless, on the phone, in the streets, in the grocery store, on the radio.

But this is the journey . . . a blessed journey . . . a fruitful journey . . . a rich journey.

It reminds me of two stories.

One is about a man seen picking up starfish that washed up on the beach after a storm and throwing them back into the water. Another man approached him, telling him there were millions of starfish on the beach, and his paltry effort couldn't possibly make any difference. The first man looked up, hurled another starfish into the ocean and replied, "It made a difference to that one!"

Then there is the story of the woman who made the beautiful altar cloth for her church. She worked on it for months and then walked barefoot for hours to deliver it because she had no shoes. The pastor saw her bloodied feet and commented about what she had suffered. She replied it was the suffering in the journey that made it such a blessed gift.

I know God is here with me and he isn't asking me for reports on how many souls were saved, or how many people were baptized, or if the church is being persecuted. He is writing each step of the journey in his Book of Life. He is carrying me on this journey when I can't carry myself anymore. He is caressing my face with the cool wind or a refreshing rainfall on a hot day.

I will fill out the reports the best I am able when people ask for them. But for me, it's the journey, not the numbers, that matter. It isn't important to me if the seed I planted one night comes to fruition in my presence because I know that God says my seeds will not return void. Johnny Appleseed didn't see every apple tree grow, but many did.

I will be satisfied with the moments on the journey, knowing that because I am here doing God's work: lives are touched, changed, and blessed.

This is not the end of the journey, it is only the beginning.

And when I reach the finish, there will be no need to take a picture because I will be in the embrace of my Savior.

And yes, we'll both be smiling . . .

Until we meet again, I leave you with these words . . .

"I only know that in every city the Holy Spirit warns me that prison and hardships are facing me. However, I consider my life worth nothing to me; my only aim is to finish the race and complete the task of testifying to the Good News of God's grace." (Acts 20:23–24 NIV)

ACKNOWLEDGEMENTS

This book is the result of a lifetime of relationships and experiences. Lee Murphree, thank you for putting up with me, always being there, and praying for me. You are an amazing husband, and I thank God we are walking this journey together.

Karen Bland, you have always encouraged me and now we run around sharing life together, watching this amazing tapestry God is weaving unfolding before our eyes.

Ashley Travis-Hall, for being the amazing gift of God that you are and for being the first person to say, "This is the next step," when I shared what I believed God was doing.

Dominic DeMasi, for showing me there is love in pain and teaching me how to be a prayerful and patient mother.

Bruce Strom, Brent Amato, and Gospel Justice Initiative, thank you for seeing the vision and for partnering with us and encouraging me. Your enthusiasm constantly ignites excitement in me. Together we are changing nations for Christ.

Thank you to the justice champions in Honduras (police, investigators, prosecutors, judges, our staff, and civilians) who work alongside us each day, fighting the good fight, working for justice, and standing in the gap. You know who you are, and so does our Father in heaven.

Also, to all of the people around this beautiful, wonderful world, who have prayed for us, come to serve with us, and who have supported us financially through the years. While God is the one who ultimately causes all of this to come to fruition, it could not have become a reality without you. You are God's hands and feet and we are forever grateful.

I desire to say thank you to "The Sistahs," who believed in me and encouraged me to write way back when my life was a mess and I didn't know who God had made me to be. You're so much a part of the story of who I am today.

And my dear sisters in our e-group "Live the Call" who allow me to be a regular person, accept me for who I am (faults and all) and who daily encourage me.

I also must thank all of you on both of my boards of directors (Honduras and United States). You have given me the freedom to hear from God and act on what he has guided us to do. You have counseled me when I needed it, chastised me when I needed it, and helped me become the leader I am today.

Thank you to all of the wonderful missionaries who serve around Honduras. You have been a blessing to me. We have walked through crises, shed tears together, and celebrated God's provision. Pastor John Mattica, thank you for stepping in to the calling to pastor us all. You have been a support, counsel, and source of strength for us.

Kathy Brown and Amy Pollick, thank you for reading my book and giving me honest feedback. Your counsel has been a tremendous help.

Mitch Chase and Jennifer Greenhill-Taylor, there are no words for me to describe how profoundly grateful I am for your editing. You are masters. From different backgrounds and perspectives, you both saw things I could not and helped me make this story so much better and tighter than I could have done without you. I am forever grateful.

Outreach Inc., Equip Press, thank you for accepting this story. Michele Tennesen, you have been such a help through this process. Your excitement about this story fueled the fire in me. Thank you for everything.

And lastly, but definitely not least, I am profoundly grateful to my Father and my Savior, for everything. This is your story. May there be more of you and less of me.

ABOUT THE AUTHOR

R. Gracie Travis-Murphree, president and co-founder of Heart of Christ-Corazon de Cristo Inc. and the Honduras Justice Project, works in Honduras teaching authorities and ministries to rescue, care for and restore victims of violence, and empower justice in one of the most dangerous countries on this earth. She wrote the first-ever program for victims of violence in Honduras at the request of the National Police in 2005. On Feb. 20, 2006, the National Police installed her as the head of the first office to attend victims of violence, commanding a team that responded to special-victims' crimes for the state of Francisco Morazan. She later also opened and became the head of offices in two additional states: Olancho and Lempira. She also served as board member and legal chair on the Honduran Children's Alliance from 2015–2017.

She has taught gospel-justice models in three countries, survived five assassination attempts, and has been an approved country condition expert on violence and gangs in Honduras and El Salvador for asylum cases in U.S. Immigration courts since 2008. Her asylum affidavit for Honduran victims of domestic violence is archived in the U.C. Hastings Center for Gender and Refugee Studies. She has spoken on immigration issues at Villanova Shool of Law and New York School of Law. She has lived in Honduras with her husband, redeeming the lost since 2005, where they have a gospel-justice center with a crisis office, refuge, and a home for girls pregnant by rape and incest.

She has received many honors in Honduras for this work, including the following: In 2009 and 2011 she received diplomas of recognition from ORHDESE (*Organizacion Hondurena para el Desarollo Social Equitativo*) for teaching the public on prevention of violence and related laws. In 2006, 2007, and 2008, the director general of the National Police issued her awards for services provided to victims of crime in Honduras. The minister of security, in 2008, gave her an award for services provided to victims of domestic violence. On Jan. 23, 2008, the president of Honduras and the minister of the National Institute of Women gave her a decoration for her work in prevention of violence for reasons of gender.

The Honduran government certified her in 2008 as a national instructor for the prevention of domestic and family violence, child and elder abuse, sexual abuse, exploitation, and human trafficking. She was also trained and certified in the investigation of sex crimes and the trafficking of women and children, execution of international investigations, and the interviewing of victims.

Gracie received a General Studies bachelor's degree from the University of North Alabama focusing on English, communications, business financial management, and justice studies. She received an award from UNA for the highest academic achievement in general studies for 2003–2004, another for the highest GPA in the 2003–2004 division, and one for outstanding academic achievement in 2002. Her internship for the degree consisted of five months during 2000 working as a news and field producer for the 5:30 a.m. newscast at WKRG TV5 (CBS) in Mobile, Alabama.

Prior to her work in Honduras, Gracie was a journalist, publishing hundreds of feature stories, articles, and columns. New York publishing houses sought her out to review their books and interview their authors for feature stories. She worked as a copy editor and writer for the *Decatur Daily* in Decatur, Alabama, wrote freelance columns for *The Boston Globe*, articles for *The Poet's Market, Wild Alabama, Mobile Bay Monthly, Mobile Press Register, The Eagle's Eye, Winchester Star,* and others. One of her articles for the *Boston Globe* on the 2000 conviction of Blanton and Cherry for the 1963 Birmingham church bombing is in the archives at the Civil Rights Museum in Birmingham, Alabama. Her poetry has been published in *The Connecticut Review, Emotions, Introspection Online, The Lyre, Buzz Nietsche, Vanguard,* and other journals.

During 2000, Gracie assisted Alabama Public Television in documentary field production for the documentary *Rebels in the Pulpit*. From 1998 through 2001, she worked as a script writer for CTN (Christian Television Network) WHBR CH 33 Pensacola/Mobile writing eighty-three weekly television shows and two mini-documentaries.

Gracie created the first online poetry group (Poet's Place) in the America Online Writer's Club in February 1997. Out of that, she created the first online poetry magazine, *Poetic Voices* and served as executive editor and publisher until 2005. She also received awards for her writing. Writer's Digest listed *Poetic Voices* as one of two poetry sites among the "101 Best Web sites for Writers" for three consecutive years: 2001, 2002, 2003. Also, in 2002 she was awarded the West Florida Literary Associations' Founder's Award for excellence in service. Among a list of other awards, she received the Lowery Varnado Poetry Award from the University of South Alabama.

Before becoming a writer and journalist, Gracie served as a foster mother for special needs children for eight years and was an advocate for women and children on The Mystic Valley Council for Children's Legislative Advocacy Committee in Winchester, Massachusetts. She was the feature speaker at two Legislative Breakfasts for Massachusetts Congressmen(women) in 1989 and 1990. She was also a feature speaker at the Massachusetts House Ways and Means Committee in advocacy of children in 1990 and received an award for advocacy for children in 1990.

Gracie has preached, taught, and spoken at hundreds of events and conferences in four countries: Honduras, Mexico, Cambodia, and the United States. Her travels and ministry have taken her to Germany, Romania, Moldova, Mexico, Guatemala, El Salvador, Honduras, and Cambodia.